The Authorities

Powerful Wisdom from Leaders in the Field

RAV BAINS

Award Winning Author

AuthoritiesPress

Publisher
Authorities Press
Markham, ON
Canada

Printed in the United States and Canada.

FOREWORD

Experts are to be admired for their knowledge, but they often remain unrecognized by the general public because they save their information and insights for paying customers and clients. There are many experts in a given field, but their impact is limited to the handful of people with whom they work.

Unlike experts, authorities share their knowledge and expertise far more broadly, so they make a big impact on the world. Authorities become known and admired as leading experts and, as such, typically do very well economically and professionally. Most authorities are also mature enough to know that part of the joy of monetary success is the accompanying moral and spiritual obligation to give back.

Many people want to learn and work with well-respected and generous authorities, but don't always know where to find them. They may be known to their peers, or within a specific community, but have not had the opportunity to reach a wider audience. At one time, they might have submitted a proposal to the For Dummies or Chicken Soup for the Soul series of books, but it's now almost impossible to get accepted as a new author in such branded book series.

It is more than fitting that Raymond Aaron, an internationally known and respected authority in his own right, would be the one to recognize the need for a new venue in which authorities could share their considerable knowledge with readers everywhere. As the only author ever to be included in both of the book series mentioned above, Raymond has had the opportunity to give back and he understands how crucial it is for authorities to have a platform from which to share their expertise.

I have known and worked with Raymond for a number of years and consider him a valued friend and talented coach. He knows how to spot talented and knowledgeable people and he desires to see them prosper. Over the years, success coaching and speaking engagements around the world have made it possible for Raymond to meet many of these talented authorities. He recognizes and relates to their passion and enthusiasm for what they do, as well as their desire to share what they know. He tells me that's why he created this new nonfiction branded book series, The Authorities.

Dr. Nido Qubein
President, High Point University

TABLE OF CONTENTS

INTRODUCTION

This book introduces you to *The Authorities* — individuals who have distinguished themselves in life and in business. Authorities make a big impact on the world. Authorities are leaders in their chosen fields. Authorities typically do very well financially, and are evolved enough to know that part of the joy of monetary success is the accompanying social, moral and spiritual obligation to give back.

Authorities are not just outstanding. They are also *known* to be outstanding.

This additional element begins to explain the difference between two strategic business and life concepts — one that seems great, but isn't, and the other that fills in the essential missing gap of the first.

The first concept is "the expert."

What is an expert? The real definition is ...

EXPERT: *a person who knows stuff*

People who have attained a very senior academic degree (like a PhD or an MD) definitely know stuff. People who read voraciously and retain what they read definitely know stuff. Unfortunately, just because you know stuff does not mean that anyone respects the fact that you do. Even though some experts are successful, alas, most are not — because knowing stuff is not enough.

Well, then, what is the missing piece?

What the expert lacks, "the authority" has. The authority both knows stuff and is *known* to know stuff. So, more simply ...

AUTHORITY: *a person who is known as an expert*

The difference is not subtle. The difference is not merely semantic. The difference is enormous.

When it comes to this subject, there are actually three categories in which people fall:

- People who don't know much and are unsuccessful in life and in business. Most people fall in this category.

- People who know stuff, but still don't leave much of a footprint in the world. There are a lot of people like this.

- Experts who are also *known* as experts become authorities and authorities are always wondrously successful. Authorities are able to contribute more to humanity through both their chosen work and their giving back.

This book is about the highest category, *The Authorities* — people who have reached the peak in their field and are known as such.

Some authorities in this book you will know. You have learned from them in the past, and you are looking forward to what they share in this book.

Rav Bains is passionate in helping and supporting people in their personal development and ensuring organizational excellence.

As you are aware, the world of work is changing at a rapid pace. Skills and abilities once considered necessary for a successful career in the workplace are now not enough. We're now coming to the realization that high IQ and well developed technical skills no longer provide a distinct advantage in the workplace. These are known as 'threshold competencies'—you need them but they won't make you a star! Breakthrough research has shown that a new measurement for determining performance in the workplace is something called Emotional Intelligence (EI). It's essential for high performance in individuals and organizations.

Recent, quiet, radical changes in our world and our work lives are ever more demanding of us if we wish to become high performing leaders. We must look to internal frontiers such as our own self-awareness, the ability to manage ourselves and others, as well as to connect with others—the basis of EI—as means of leveraging performance.

The purpose of Rav Bain's chapter is to provide you with an engaging experience based on the powerful and practical applications of EI. Specifically, it will serve to enhance your personal leadership skills.

Ultimately, Rav's chapter will help you and those in your agency to better understand your emotions and provide a series of practical techniques and tools to manage them more effectively.

The goal here is to help you increase your personal leadership abilities by beginning to master the competencies of EI. This will assist you and others to achieve the greatest potential.

At the end of Rav's chapter you'll be able to:

- Understand EI and its value to you personally and professionally

- Learn and practice techniques to manage your own and others' emotions more skillfully

- Understand why this is important for your organization

They are *The Authorities*. Learn from them. Connect with them. Let them uplift you. Learning from them and working with them is the secret ingredient for success which may well allow you to rise to the level of Authority soon.

To be considered for inclusion in a subsequent edition of *The Authorities*, register to attend a future event at www.aaron.com/events where you will be interviewed and considered.

Unlocking the Secret to Success

Discovering the Power of Emotional Intelligence

RAV BAINS

WHAT IS EMOTIONAL INTELLIGENCE?

What is an emotion?

An emotion is a feeling we get as a result of something that has triggered us. This trigger can be internal or external; in other words, something that we think, see, hear, speak or do. For example, you might see two people arguing, and that could arouse some emotion in you. An example of an internal trigger could be that you think of something in the past that was negative, and this has brought up an emotion in you. The other important factor to remember is that an emotion can be strong or weak. The strength of the emotion will depend on your interpretation of what you've thought, seen, heard, spoke or done. Since we all have different values and belief systems, the event, whether internal or external, is "neutral." Why is this important to understand? Because you have a choice as to how to react to the thing that has happened! Now you might ask how this is possible. If I see a car accident how can that be neutral? Isn't it bound to evoke an emotion? Well, what is the likelihood that ten people who witnessed the accident will have the same reaction? They won't. Their reactions could range from very strong to slight, to no reaction at all. So, it's not the event, but rather your interpretation of that event that will determine the emotion. One of the reasons you blame the event for your emotional reaction is that it all happens in a fraction of a second! As a result, you confuse the trigger (the event) with your emotional reaction, which is actually determined by you. This topic always becomes an interesting conversational point in my seminars, which is great because it allows for rich understanding of emotions and triggers. The important thing to remember is that life has no meaning until we give it meaning.

What triggers an emotion?

Now that we have touched on emotions and triggers, the next critical question for you to ask is what triggers your emotions. Understanding this question is fundamental to understanding your personal and professional success or failure. You see, people never stop to think why they have an emotional reaction to something. In fact, did you know that 90% of the population don't think? (Earl Nightingale) Just because they have thoughts (which are often haphazard), they believe they are thinking. Thinking is the deliberate, conscious awareness of the thoughts you are having, and deciding what thoughts you actually want to have. The other fundamental mistake people make is that they think they are their thoughts. We aren't our thoughts. We are aware of our thoughts, so we can't be the thoughts. Now at this point you might feel a little confused.

That's ok, it will become clearer as you read on. It's critical that you get to know what triggers you. It could be what people say or do, or certain circumstances, situations or events. It's also important to be aware of the type of emotion or feeling you're getting in those situations and circumstances. These emotions will determine how you act and react. Are they positive or negative? Are they pleasurable or painful? These questions will help to determine whether you're making good judgments or not. They will also determine whether you're responding or reacting to the person, situation or circumstances. One of the other fundamental factors to remember is that human beings can trigger an emotional reaction simply by thinking bad thoughts—without anyone else interfering. So, you can get into a bad mood all by yourself!

Emotions Drive Behavior

Many people seem to think that their circumstances cause them to react to things, and that's why they have an emotional reaction. As a result, they constantly blame what's happening around them, which is external to them. In my coaching sessions I've heard so many individuals complain about their partner, the kids, the boss or their team at work. It's as if they think that changing what's around them will allow them to be happy or in a better mood. This means no more emotional reaction. Well, if you've been following the earlier reading, then you'll have remembered that all events are neutral, and only you are in control of your feelings and emotions. Therefore, the mood you're in or the emotional reaction you're having to a situation or event will determine how you behave! For example, if you're in a bad mood, what's the likelihood you're going to be at your best at home or in the workplace? We can safely assume you're not going to be! What many people fail to realize is that emotions, not circumstances, drive behavior. So, how you're feeling or what kind of emotional state you're in will determine your performance and your leadership. This means that if you want to change your own or someone else's behavior you must get to the root cause of the emotion that's driving them or you, otherwise you'll be focusing your energies on the symptoms instead of causes and, as a result, be less effective in your efforts. This is one of the key elements to understand as part of EI.

Definition of EI

Now that we've established what emotions are, what triggers emotions and that emotions drive behavior, we can conclude that *EI is one's ability to understand one's emotions—what triggers them, what circumstances cause the trigger and how to regulate the emotions.* By doing this there is a good chance that you'll make better, more thoughtful decisions and have a positive impact on those around you. This means better performance by you, and the role modeling of good personal leadership.

WHAT IS WISDOM?

Wisdom is having the knowledge of what is right or true, coupled with just judgment regarding an action to be taken. The most famous example of this is the story of two women who came to King Solomon, each claiming to be the mother of a certain infant. Knowing that only one could be the true mother, King Solomon decreed that the baby be cut in half and one part given to each woman. The true mother, unwilling to have her baby hurt in any way, revoked her claim. Solomon knew this would happen and, thus, awarded the child to that woman.

Intelligence versus Wisdom

King Solomon had to understand intelligence in order to make the decision he did ... He had to be prepared to go through with his decree. And he also had to know how the true mother would react. So, on the surface, it would seem that both intelligence and emotional intelligence are necessary for wisdom. However, if we accept that the two women were intelligent in their own way, it quickly becomes apparent that intelligence is not necessary for wisdom.

Why is this important?

Thinking is the deliberate, conscious awareness of the thoughts you're having and then deciding what thoughts you want to have. This is the exact opposite of what most people do. Most people base their actions on how they feel in the moment. They don't take time to rationalize the situation and choose an appropriate thought.

WHY DO ORGANIZATIONS NEED EMOTIONAL INTELLIGENCE?

Because there are:

- **Challenges in individual behavior** ... Once Emotional Intelligence is understood by individuals in organizations, their behavior changes dramatically. They stop reacting and start to respond thoughtfully to situations.

- **Challenges in building relationships** … If employees are unable to cooperate with each other, this will affect organizational performance. Once people start to grasp the concept and competences of self-awareness, cooperation and harmony, it will lead to better results.

- **Challenges in teamwork** … Teamwork is critical for success; however, too often individuals in teams fall into the "right wrong trap!" and individuals quickly start to take positions. Once people understand that it's all emotional, they start to focus on outcomes and results.

- **Challenges in managing change** … Organizations struggle in implementing change, and employees often resist. Fear is a big factor in change management, as people focus on what they will lose as opposed to what they will gain. People start to 'awfulize,' but once they understand that it's the relationship between the emotional mind and the thinking mind that is driving the fear, resistance disappears.

- **Challenges in achieving organizational goals** … Employees often struggle with their values versus the organization's values. They often forget what their Personal Leadership Responsibility is in the organization. Understanding the philosophy of Emotional Intelligence and personal accountability puts them back on the right track.

- **Challenges in understanding 'soft skills!'** … Organizations spend millions of dollars on driving hard for goals and results, but remain weak on developing the soft skills required by individuals and teams. They fail to realize that it's the 'soft stuff' that makes the 'hard stuff' easier! Once individuals and teams grasp this concept, they excel in all areas of their lives and get engaged actively in achieving organizational results.

The main thing to remember about Emotional Intelligence is that it can be taught, improved and used within your company to create a healthy workplace, motivate employees and achieve your goals. It's definitely a strong tool that can put you out in front of your competition. So, get from being a good organization to a great organization!

UNDERSTANDING EMOTIONS AS VIBRATIONS

One of the failures of our learning is that no one has explained to us that emotions are actual vibrations in the body. When we are angry, we don't say "I have a negative vibration" we say "I am angry!" In other words, we have made the emotion part of who we are and, as a result, we do not pay attention to the vibration. We don't realize that it's a vibration, and that we aren't our vibrations. We are aware of our vibrations. I know this might be a little confusing, BUT this is one of the keys to really grasping what is happening to us emotionally. As a result, we'll have a chance to manage our emotions and hence our behavior.

It's critical to be in tune with what is happening in the body, and paying attention when there is a change in this vibration, because then you'll know you're having a reaction to something. I can't stress enough the importance of this fact. Start paying attention to the sensations/vibrations in your body. Stop living from the neck upwards, just in the mind!

I believe you aren't going to get this important piece of information from any other emotional intelligence book or trainer.

THINK ABOUT WHAT YOU'RE THINKING

We very rarely pay any attention to our thoughts. The average person doesn't understand the importance of thinking. People assume this is an activity that just happens and that they really don't have any control over it. Wrong! If you want to change your life, then start paying attention to what you're constantly thinking about. Are your thoughts negative or positive? Why is this important? Well, thoughts arouse emotions. Earl Nightingale, in 1960, said that "90% of people simply don't think!" You see, you need to understand that activity in the mind isn't thinking. We're constantly thinking about shopping lists, work, picking the kids up, cooking, and on and on we go! Not that this isn't important, but you need to understand that you're not your thoughts. You are, however, aware of your thoughts and therefore can choose what you think about. Negative thoughts will trigger negative emotions. Conversely, positive thoughts will trigger positive emotions, which in turn puts us in a better state of mind. We as humans have so habituated negative thinking that we have normalized it. So we pay no attention to what we're thinking and how it is affecting our behavior and performance. Understanding the importance of your thoughts, which give rise to emotions, is critical in changing your behavior. Managing your thinking and your emotions will lead to better management of your behavior. Remember, thoughts arouse emotions.

What is thinking?

Thinking is conscious and it's active. Think of it as internal speech (requires language). Sometimes that inner conversation appears to come unbidden or automatically; this would be subconscious thought. But it is during conscious and active thought that thinking takes on a whole new role. Here we can focus our thoughts to solve a problem. We can plan, design and, quite literally, create. This is where we can purposefully produce our thoughts and put some form to them. In simpler words, thinking is the action of using one's mind to produce thoughts.

90% of the People Don't Think

It's true; most people don't think. They go through their days on automatic, their thoughts being a reaction to what's happening around them and to them, rather than being a purposeful response. No wonder, though. The Socratic method is no longer taught in schools, and the young people of today don't seem to understand the importance of the "question." If you ask yourself (your mind) a question, the mind will always answer. Ask a great question, and you'll always get a great response. In fact, it's the act of questioning that creates our thoughts. So, think what will happen to a person who doesn't understand the importance of questions. Something happens, and random, or at least reactive, thoughts appear. Negative questions abound. *Why is this happening to me? What's going on? Who does he think he is? Where does this leave me?* Get the picture? What if this person had responded rather than reacted? The questions asked might appear like this: *This is interesting: how can what's happening serve me? Do I understand the situation properly, or will he clarify it for me? He certainly has some strong opinions: I wonder what his experience is in this area and if he would be interested in sharing his story and his reasoning? I think I'll ask him. Can't hurt, right?*

Why is this important?

The questions we ask will determine what we say and do. They are like the programs we feed our computer so that it can manipulate the raw data it receives in a way that is useful to us. You're the operator or programmer of your mind. You don't want to fall asleep on the job, do you? Then learn to ask yourself questions designed to get your mind used to generating specific words and actions so that they become a habit you can call on in many different situations. I call them rituals.

Thoughts Arouse Emotions

One of the most wonderful aspects of thought is that it can arouse emotions. You can discover which words or thoughts elicit emotions that can work for you in a difficult situation, then you can practice calling up those emotions. I'm talking about positive emotions like excitement, joy, happiness, and peace.

COMPETENCES OF EMOTIONAL INTELLIGENCE

There are many different views and opinions on the competences of Emotional Intelligence. I've found the following to be the best examples to describe the important competences.

Self-awareness is the foundation on which all other competences build on. Often, we don't take the time to disengage from day-to-day activity to review what has happened to us.

Example ... Before you go to bed at night, take the time to review your day. Ask questions like: *What were the positives? Which of my goals were achieved? What happened to make the day memorable?* Once you feel your review is complete, set your mind to work, planning tomorrow's day. You should write your goals down.

Example ... How can you really understand your stress levels if you don't spend some quiet time posing and answering questions designed to put your focus on the stress you feel in each large muscle mass? So, think back to a time when you felt totally relaxed and the stress literally bled from your body. What did that feel like? Compare that feeling to the one in the muscle mass we've been talking about. Clench those muscles for a count of ten and release. Does the feeling in the muscles match what you remembered? Not quite? Clench the muscles for another 10 seconds and release. Immediately notice how the muscles feel. Now do this with all the large muscles in your body, beginning with your head and working downward to your feet.

Make sure you're doing your best to match the feeling of relaxation you remembered. Breathe in when you clench, breathe out when you release. You can even pretend you're releasing the air through the muscle you just released. Do you feel yourself settling into your chair or your bed? Keep practicing and one day soon you'll find yourself completely relaxed.

Self-assessment is the ability to honestly assess one's strengths and weakness. This has to be done skillfully. It's an opportunity to review what you're naturally good at and what the opportunities are for self-improvement. Self-assessment does not mean beating yourself up! But, rather, it's thoughtful self-reflection that adds value in increasing your awareness about yourself and how you interact with your environment.

Again, use questions to elicit the thoughts you're after. *What did I do well today? What skills and talents did I use? What could I have done better? How?*

Managing Emotion

I've heard emotion referred to as a wild stallion that must be tamed. Thoughts generate emotions; emotions generate thoughts. Of the two possibilities, which seems more useful to you? Thoughts generating emotions, right? You have the reins: it's up to you to teach the stallion what that means, that you're in control.

It's much easier to choose useful thoughts that generate positive, supporting emotions than it is to control the thoughts evoked by powerful, negative emotions. Think about it … you always have a choice. You can ask questions that create thoughts that will evoke useful emotions or you can be overrun by thoughts that boil up unbidden from out of control negative emotion. You can tame the wild stallion or it can cast you into the dirt.

How is this emotion working for me? What thoughts can I choose that will evoke a better emotional response? What's good about this situation, and how can it serve me? Such questions are designed to focus on positive thoughts, emotions and results rather than reacting blindly to whatever emotion is elicited by the situation at hand.

Emotional Intelligence can be taught, improved and used within your company to achieve your goals. It is definitely a strong tool that can put you out in front of your competition. For more information or to book a seminar for your company, contact me at **ravsbains1@gmail.com.**

FINAL NOTE

The most important thing you can take away from this chapter is: **Life has no meaning other than what we give it**. A woman at a party stumbles and falls. One person is concerned that the woman might have been hurt by the fall. A second person starts laughing (because he noticed that the contents of the woman's drink flew into the face of someone he doesn't like very much).

In this situation, a woman fell. This has no meaning without context, hence the reactions of the two witnesses. They both put the fall into a specific context and then assigned meaning. The first witness saw the fall in the context of the woman becoming injured. This triggered the emotion of concern. The second witness saw the fall in the context of someone he disliked getting a drink in the face. This triggered the emotion of delight.

The trick, the wisdom we must develop, is understanding that we have FREE WILL to choose whatever it is we want to think, feel, say or do. It doesn't matter what has happened, because it means nothing until, and if, we make it so.

Remember ... "People will often forget what you said, but they will never forget how you made them feel." - Maya Angelou

To book a seminar for your organization, contact
Rav Bains at **ravsbains1@gmail.com**

Step Into Greatness

LES BROWN

You have greatness within you. You can do more than you could ever imagine. The problem most people have is that they set a goal and then ask, "how can I do it? I don't have the necessary skills or education or experience."

I know what that's like. I wasted 14 years on asking myself how I could be a motivational speaker. My mind focused on the negative—on the things that were in my way, rather than on the things that were not.

It's not what you don't have but what you think you need that keeps you from getting what you want from life. But, when the dream is big enough, the obstacles don't matter. You'll get there if you stay the course. Nothing can stop you but death itself.

Think about that last statement for a minute. There's nothing on this earth that can stop you from achieving what it is that you want. So, get out of your way, and quit sabotaging your dreams. Do everything in your power to make them happen—because you cannot fail!

They say the best way to die is with your loved ones gathered around your bed. But what if you were dying and it was the ideas you never acted upon, the gifts you never used and the dreams you never pursued, that were circled around your bed? Answer that question right now. Write down your answers. If you die this very moment, what ideas, what gifts, what dreams will die with you?

Then say: I refuse to die an unlived life! You beat out 40 million sperm to get here, and you'll never have to face such odds again. Walk through the field of life and leave a trail behind.

One day, one of my rich friends brought my mother a new pair of shoes for me. Now, even though we weren't well off, I didn't want them; they were a size nine and I was a size nine and a half. My mother didn't listen and told my sister to go get some Vaseline, which she rubbed all over my feet. Then my mother had me put those shoes on, minding that I didn't scrunch down the heel. She had my sister run some water in the bathtub, and I was told to get in and walk around in the water. I said that my feet hurt. She just ignored me and asked about my day at school, how everything went and did I get into any fights? I knew what she was up to, that she was trying to distract me, so I said I had only gotten into three fights. After a while mother asked me if my feet still hurt. I admitted that the pain had indeed lessened. She kept me walking in that tub until I had a brand new pair of comfortable, size nine and a half shoes.

You see, once the leather in the shoes got wet, they stretched! And what you need to do is stretch a little. I believe that most people don't set high goals and miss them, but rather, they set lower goals and hit them and then they stay there, stuck on the side of the highway of life. When you're pursuing your greatness, you don't know what your limitations are, and you need to act like you don't have any. If you shoot for the moon and miss, you'll still be in the stars.

You also need coaching (a mentor). Why? There are times you, too, will find yourself parked on the side of the highway of life with no gas in the vehicle. What you need then is someone to stop and offer to pick up some gas down the road a ways and bring it back to you. That person is your coach. Yes, they are there for advice, but their main job is to help you through the difficulties that life throws at all of us.

Another reason for having a coach is that you can't see the picture when you're in the frame. In other words, he or she can often see where you are with a clarity and focus that's unavailable to you. They're not going to leave you parked along the road of life, nor are they going to allow you to be stuck in the moment like a photo in a frame.

And let's say you just can't see your way forward. You don't believe it's possible. Sometimes you just have to believe in someone's belief in you. This could be your coach, a loved one, or even a staunch friend. You need to hear them say you can do it, time and again. Because, after all, faith comes from hearing and hearing and hearing.

Look at it this way. Most people fail because of possibility blindness. They can't see what lies before them. There are always possibilities. Because of this, your dream is possible. You may fail often. In fact, I want you to say this: I will fail my way to success. Here is why.

I had a TV show that failed. I felt I had to go back to public speaking. I had failed, so I parked my car for 10 years. Then I saw Dr. Wayne Dyer was still on PBS and I decided to call them. They said they would love to work with me and asked where I had been. I wasn't as good as I had been 10 years before, as I was out of practice, but I still had to get back in the game. I was determined to drive on empty.

Listen to recordings, go to seminars, challenge yourself, and you'll begin to step into your greatness; you'll begin to fill yourself with the energy you need to climb to ever greater heights. Most people never attend a seminar. They won't invest money in books or audio programs. You put yourself in the top 5 percent just by making a different choice than the average person. This is called contrary thinking. It's a concept taken from the financial industry. One considers choosing the exact opposite behaviour of the average person as a way to get better than average results. You don't have to make the contrarian choice, but if you don't have anything to lose by going that road, why not consider the option?

Make your move before you're ready. Walk by faith, not by sight, and make sure you're happy doing it. If you can't be happy, what else is there? Helen Keller said, "Life is short, eat the dessert first."

What is faith? Many of us think of God when we think of faith. A different viewpoint claims that faith is a firm belief in something for which there is no proof. I would rather think of faith as something that is believed especially with strong conviction. It is this last definition I am referring to when I say walk by faith, not by sight. Be happy and go forth with strong conviction that you are destined for greatness.

An important step on your way to greatness is to take the time to detoxify. You've got to look at the people in your life. What are they doing for you? Are they setting a pace that you can follow? If not, whose pace have you adjusted to? If you're the smartest in your group, find a new group.

Are the people in your life pulling you down or lifting you up? You know what to do, right? Banish the negative and stay with the positive; it's that simple. Dr. Norman Vincent Peale once said (when I was in the audience), "You are special. You have greatness within you, and you can do more than you could ever possibly imagine."

He overrode the inner conversations in my mind and reached the heart of me. He set me on fire. This is yet another reason for seeking out the help of a coach or mentor, or other new people in your life. They can do what Dr. Peale did for me. They can set your passion free.

How important is it to have the right kind of person/people on your side? There was a study done that determined it takes 16 people saying you can do something to overcome one person who says you can't do something. That's right, one negative, unsupportive person can wipe out the work of 16 other supportive people. The message can't be any clearer than that.

Let's face the cold, hard truth: most people stay in park along the highway of life. They never feel the passion, the love for their fellow man, or for the work they do. They are stuck in the proverbial rut. What's the reason? There are many reasons, but only one common factor: fear—fear of change, fear of failure, fear of success, fear they may not be good enough, fear of competition, even fear of rejection.

"Rejection is a myth," says Jack Canfield, co-author of The Chicken Soup for the Soul series. "It's not like you get a slap in the face each time you are rejected." Why not take every "no" you receive as a vitamin, and every time you take one, know you are another step closer to success.

You will win if you don't quit. Even a broken clock is right twice a day.

Professional baseball players, on average, get on base just three times out of every 10 times they face the opposing pitcher. Even superstars fail half of the time they appear at the plate.

Top commissioned salespeople face similar odds. They may make one sale from every three people they see, but it will have taken them between 75 and 100 telephone calls to make the 15 appointments they need to close their five sales for the week. And these are statistics for the elite. Most salespeople never reach these kinds of numbers.

People don't spend their lives working for just one company anymore. This means you must build up a set of skills and experiences that are portable. This can be done a number of ways, but my favorite approaches follow.

You must be willing to do the things others won't do, in order to have tomorrow the things that others don't have. Provide more service than you get paid for. Set some high standards for yourself.

Begin each day with your most difficult task. The rest of the day will seem more enjoyable and a whole lot easier.

Someone needs help with a problem? Be the solution to that problem.

Also, find those tasks that are being consistently ignored and do them. You'll be surprised by the results. An acquaintance of mine used this approach at a number of entry-level positions and each time he quickly ended up being offered a position in management.

You must increase your energy. Kick it up a notch. We are spirits having a physical existence; let your spirit shine. Quit frittering away your energy. Use it to move you closer to the achievement of your dreams. Refuse to spend it on non-productive activities.

What do people say about you when you leave a room? Are you willing to take responsibility—to walk your talk. There is a terrible epidemic sweeping our nation, and it is the refusal to take responsibility for one's actions. Consider that at some point in any situation there will have been a moment where you could have done something to change the outcome. To that end, you are responsible for what happened. It's a hard thing to accept, but it's true.

Life's hard. It was hard when I was told I had cancer. I had sunken into despair, and was hiding away in my study when my son came in. My son asked me if I was going to die. What could I do? I told him I was going to fight, even though I was scared. I also told him that I needed some help. Not because I was weak, but because I wanted to stay strong. Keep asking until you get help. Don't stop until you get it.

A setback is the setup for a comeback. A setback is simply a misstep on the long road of success. It means nothing in the larger scheme of things. And, surprisingly, it sets you up for your next win. It tends to focus you and your energy on your immediate goals, paving the way for your next sprint, for your comeback.

It's worth it. Your dreams are worth the sacrifices you'll have to make to achieve them. Find five reasons that will make your dreams worth it for you. Say to yourself, I refuse to live an unlived life.

If you are casual about your dreams, you'll end up a casualty. You must be passionate about your dreams, living and breathing them throughout your days. You've got to be hungry! People who are hungry refuse to take no for an answer. Make NO your vitamin. Be unstoppable. Be hungry.

Let me give you an example of what I mean by hungry …

I decided I wanted to become a disc jockey, so I went down to the local radio station and asked the manager, Mr. Milton "Butterball" Smith, if he had a job available for a disc jockey. He said he did not. The next day I went back, and Mr. Smith asked, "Weren't you here yesterday?" I explained that I was just checking to see if anyone was sick or had died. He responded by telling me not to come back again. Day three, I went back again—with the same story. Mr. Smith told me to get out of there. I came back the fourth day and gave Mr. Smith my story one more time. He was so beside himself that he told me to get him a cup of coffee. I said, "Yes, sir!" That's how I became the errand boy.

While working as an errand boy at the station, I took every opportunity to hang out with the disc jockeys and to observe them working. After I had taught myself how to run the control room, it was just a matter of biding my time.

Then one day an opportunity presented itself. One of the disc jockeys by the name of Rockin' Roger was drinking heavily while he was on the air. It was a Saturday afternoon. And there I was, the only one there.

I watched him through the control-room window. I walked back and forth in front of that window like a cat watching a mouse, saying "Drink, Rock, Drink!" I was young. I was ready. And I was hungry.

Pretty soon, the phone rang. It was the station manager. He said, "Les, this is Mr. Klein."

I said, "Yes, I know."

He said, "Rock can't finish his program."

I said, "Yes sir, I know."

He said, "Would you call one of the other disc jockeys to fill in?"

I said, "Yes sir, I sure will, sir."

And when he hung up, I said, "Now he must think I'm crazy." I called up my mama and my girlfriend, Cassandra, and I told them, "Ya'll go out on the front porch and turn up the radio, I'M ABOUT TO COME ON THE AIR!"

I waited 15 or 20 minutes and called the station manager back. I said, "Mr. Klein, I can't find NOBODY!"

He said, "Young boy, do you know how to work the controls?"

I said, "Yes, sir."

He said, "Go in there, but don't say anything. Hear me?"

I said, "Yes, sir."

I couldn't wait to get old Rock out of the way. I went in there, took my seat behind that turntable, flipped on the microphone, and let 'er rip.

"Look out, this is me, LB., triple P. Les Brown your platter-playin' papa. There were none before me and there will be none after me, therefore that makes me the one and only. Young and single and love to mingle, certified, bona fide, and indubitably qualified to bring you satisfaction and a whole lot of action. Look out baby, I'm your LOVE man."

I WAS HUNGRY!

During my adult life, I've been a disc jockey, a radio station manager, a Democrat in the Ohio Legislature, a minister, a TV personality, an author, and a public speaker, but I've always looked after what I valued most—my mother. What I want for her is one of my dreams, one of my goals.

My life has been a true testament to the power of positive thinking and the infinite human potential. I was born in an abandoned building on a floor in Liberty City, a low-income section of Miami, Florida, and adopted at six weeks of age by Mrs. Mamie Brown, a 38-year-old single woman, cafeteria cook, and domestic worker. She had very little education or financial means, but a very big heart and the desire to care for myself and my twin brother. I call myself Mrs. Mamie Brown's Baby Boy and I say that all that I am and all that I ever hoped to be, I owe to my mother.

My determination and persistence in searching for ways to help my mother overcome poverty, and developing my philosophy to do whatever it takes to achieve success, led me to become a distinguished authority on harnessing human potential and success. That philosophy is best expressed by the following ...

"If you want a thing bad enough to go out and fight for it,
to work day and night for it,
to give up your time, your peace, and your sleep for it...
if all that you dream and scheme is about it,
and life seems useless and worthless without it...
if you gladly sweat for it and fret for it and plan for it
and lose all your terror of the opposition for it...
if you simply go after that thing you want
with all of your capacity, strength, and sagacity,
faith, hope and confidence and stern pertinacity...
if neither cold, poverty, famine, nor gout,
sickness nor pain, of body, and brain,
can keep you away from the thing that you want...
if dogged and grim you beseech and beset it,
with the help of God, you will get it!"

The 3 Things You Need to Become a Real Estate Millionaire

The Right Way to Invest Successfully

RAYMOND AARON

It seems like everywhere you look, someone is claiming that they became a millionaire by investing in real estate, and encouraging you to do the same. There are lots of TV shows about flipping houses for a fast buck that make it appear as if it's easy to find the right property and just as easy to sell it in a matter of months for a good profit. Unfortunately, that's not really how it works.

Investing in real estate is a proven way to make money, a lot of it. You could end up with millions, but you could also make a lot of very costly mistakes along the way. There has been so much hype about how easy it is to become a real estate millionaire that many people jump into the market without knowing what they are doing, and that's a shame, especially because qualified help is available.

Anyone can invest successfully in real estate if they have three things: a great real estate mentor, a proven real estate system, and a way to correctly predict the future. In other words, you need someone smart and knowledgeable to guide you; an understanding of the financial and legal aspects of buying, holding, and selling real estate; and an ability to see societal trends and visualize how those trends will impact the real estate market.

A GREAT REAL ESTATE MENTOR

Investing on your own can be financially dangerous, especially for a first-timer. You're dealing with a lot of money, so any mistake can be a huge one. Buying at the wrong time in the cycle can kill your investments. And, regardless of the real estate strategy you employ, you're bound to hold onto properties for some period of time which means that severe negative cash flow and vacancies can ruin you. Plus, bad property management and a failure to know the most recent real estate and tax laws can get you sued.

An experienced mentor can help you choose the best real estate strategies for your situation, and the right properties in which to invest. They can also help you avoid the many possible pitfalls and make money while holding properties, and counsel you on when to sell for a great profit. Working with the right mentor can also keep real estate investing from becoming your full-time job.

Many people find that some part of the investment process is uncomfortable for them, whether it's initiating a conversation with a realtor, submitting an offer, or hiring a property manager. A mentor can be very helpful in such situations as well.

In sum, learning from and working with the right mentor can make you a highly profitable investor in a relatively short period of time. Look for someone with years of experience and a proven track record.

A PROVEN SYSTEM

There's much more to investing in real estate than "buy low, sell high." To be successful, you must have the correct facts and the correct monthly habits concerning your real estate. Overall, you need to know what to buy, when to buy it, whether there will be a positive cash flow while you're holding on to it, and when to sell. Plus, what is the right low? What is the right high? How much money do you have to put down and how much income must be generated while you're waiting to sell?

Determining if a property is a good buy takes a lot of research and analysis. You will need to look at comparable purchase prices in the area, as well as rental fees. You'll also need to consider the location, the age and condition of the building, tax rates, and about 30 other pieces of data. Evaluating the information for just one property could take you a day or more.

If you're serious about becoming a real estate investor, you are going to be considering quite a lot of properties on a regular basis. Even if you want to make investing your day job, you'll never have the time necessary to research fully and evaluate every property that comes to your attention. Hence, the first part of your system has to involve weeding out the lesser opportunities and focusing on the ones with potential.

The investors I mentor learn how to determine if a property is really a great deal in seconds. You only need two pieces of data: the purchase price and the current rent rate. Compare the two using a two-part formula. First, divide the asking price (outgoing funds) by 100. Then, given that current mortgage interest rates are below 8-10% divide the number you got by two. If the current monthly rent doesn't meet or better that second number, eliminate the property from consideration.

As an example, say the asking price is $1,000,000. If you divide it by 100, it comes out to $10,000. Divide again, by two, and you get $5,000. If the monthly rent isn't $5,000 or more, you should pass on the property. You may miss out on a few winners using this system but, if you eliminate more properties than you think you should, you'll be successful and safe. Remember that, if interest rates rise significantly, you will need to adjust the formula to compensate.

Once you've weeded out the chaff from the wheat, do your due diligence on the remaining properties. Work closely with your mentor during this part of the process and, again, when it comes to making deals, say no more than you say yes. Just don't get cold feet or shy away from a great deal.

In terms of timing, it all comes down to momentum. There is always an overall upward momentum. Real estate prices go up and down, on an upwards track. So, one good profit strategy is to buy low, watch values rise and sell during the next boom. More precisely, you want to buy just as prices rise off the bottom (so that they're already rising) and sell when prices hit double the bottom, which is typically the very minimum prices rise to at the peak of the ensuing boom.

Don't attempt to predict the extremes—you will make a significant amount of money more safely buying just after prices begin rising (not the lowest point) and selling towards the end of the up period—without the risk associated with waiting too long and missing the highest point.

You'll also need a system for monitoring your investments while holding on until it's time to sell. Having a strong property manager is essential. So is reviewing rents taken in versus uncollectibles, repairs, and other expenses to ensure that your cash flow remains positive.

PREDICTING THE FUTURE

Good real estate investors learn to identify marketplace trends and buyers' or renters' needs. Start by investigating and tracking growth trends by neighborhood: are prices rising, is an area getting ready for a renaissance, are there new job opportunities nearby, or is the area close to another neighborhood that's gotten too pricey?

Great real estate investors, however, go far beyond those basics. They look for large demographic or social elements that might provide the next big opportunity. The huge number of returning veterans after World War II led to a Baby Boom that provides the perfect example. Every stage of their lives brought an opportunity for marketers, real estate builders, and other manufacturers to fill unmet needs, be it starter homes for when they had children, tricycles for those children who were too young to ride a bike, or new sizes and types of cars. All of this was predictable, but no one noticed. Opportunities were capitalized upon as they arose, but imagine what financial success could have been attained if someone had predicted the Baby Boomers' needs in advance.

And, now, those Boomers are driving the growth of retirement communities and nursing homes. But, they are a more independent lot than their parents were, and have strived to remain young and healthy as long as possible. Quite a few of them can still live and thrive on their own, but many may need a little help at this point in their lives. They don't need or want an aide, nurse, or social worker on a full-time basis, and certainly aren't ready for a nursing home. That means there is a huge need for more up-to-date, internet-ready independent supportive living arrangements, of which there are too few. Investing in one now is bound to be a win.

Don't forget that those Baby Boomers had children of their own, and that created a mini baby boom. Think about the ways in which those children, now middle-aged adults, are different from their parents and what needs they might have, especially regarding real estate. You might also consider whether changes in the workforce, higher divorce rates, and the economics of leaving home after college have implications for the real estate market as well. Keep your eyes and minds open!

If you would like to learn more about winning strategies for investing in real estate, please visit http://rarestmonthlymentor.com.

Sex, Love and Relationships

DR. JOHN GRAY

Just as great sex is important to lasting love, good health is important to sex and relationships. About 12 years ago, I cured myself of early stage Parkinson's disease. The doctors were amazed, but my wife was even more amazed. She noted that our relationship and sex life had become dramatically better. It turns out that the natural supplements I used to reverse Parkinson's can also make you more attentive and loving in your relationship. At that point, I realized that good relationship skills alone were not enough to sustain love and passion for a lifetime.

31

I shared many insights gained from my 40 years' experience as a marriage counselor and coach in *Men Are From Mars, Women Are From Venus*. And while my insights go a long way towards helping men and women understand and support each other, good communication skills alone are not always enough. For better relationships, we not only need to be healthy, but we must also experience optimum brain function.

If you are tired, depressed, anxious, not sleeping well, or in pain, then certainly romantic feelings will become a thing of the past. My recovery from Parkinson's revealed to me the profound connection between the quality of our health and our relationships. This insight has motivated me, over the past twelve years, to research the secrets of optimum health as a foundation for lasting love.

These are health secrets that are generally not explored in medical school. In medical school, doctors are indoctrinated into the culture of examining the symptoms, identifying the sickness, and prescribing a drug to treat that sickness. They learn very little about how to be healthy or to sustain successful relationships.

There are no university courses entitled "Better Nutrition For Better Sex". Drugs sometimes save lives, but they also have negative side effects that do little to preserve the passion in a relationship. Ideally, drugs should be used as a last resort and 90 % of our health plan should be drug free. From this perspective, the heath care crisis, as well as our high rate of divorce in America, is indirectly caused by our dependence on doctors and prescription drugs.

Most people have not even considered that taking prescribed drugs (even for the small stuff) can weaken their relationships, which in turn makes them more vulnerable to more disease. For example, if you are feeling depressed or anxious, a drug may numb your pain, but it does nothing to help you correct the cause of your problem. It can even prevent you from feeling your natural motivation to get the emotional support you need. In a variety of ways, our common health complaints are all expressions of two major conditions: our lack of education to identify and support unmet gender-specific emotional needs; and our lack of education to identify and support unmet gender-specific nutritional needs.

With an understanding of natural solutions that have been around for thousands of years, drugs are not needed to treat many common complaints. Some symptoms like low energy, weight gain, allergies, hormonal imbalance, mood swings, poor sleep, indigestion, lack of focus, ADD and ADHD, procrastination, low motivation, memory loss, decreased libido, PMS, vaginal dryness, muscle and joint pain, or the lack of passion in life and/or our relationships can be treated drug-free. By using drugs (even over-the-counter drugs) to treat these common complaints, our bodies and relationships are weakened, making us more vulnerable to bigger and more costly health challenges like cancer, diabetes, heart disease, auto-immune disease, dementia, and Alzheimer's. In simple terms, by handling the easy stuff (the common complaints) without doctors and drugs, we can protect ourselves from the big stuff (cancer, heart disease, dementia, etc.) We can be healthy and also enjoy lasting love and passion in our personal lives.

Even if you are taking anti-depressants or hormone replacement therapy, sometimes all it takes to stop treating the symptom is to directly handle the cause. With specific mineral orotates (something most people have never heard of) or omega three oil from the brains of salmon, your stress levels immediately drop and you begin to feel happy and in love again.

For every health challenge, we have explored the effects on our relationships, with as well as natural remedies that can sometimes produce immediate positive results. You can find these natural solutions to common health complaints for free at my website: www.MarsVenus.com.

What they don't teach in medical school is how to be healthy and happy without the use of drugs or hormone replacement. By refusing drugs and taking responsibility for your health, a wealth of new possibilities can become available to you. We are designed to be healthy and happy, and it is within our reach if we commit to increasing our knowledge.

New research regarding the brain differences in men and women reveals how specific nutritional supplements, combined with gender-specific relationship and self-nurturing skills, can stimulate the hormones of health, happiness and increased energy. Over the past 10 years in my healing center in California, I witnessed how natural solutions coupled with gender-specific relationship skills could solve our common health complaints without drugs. By addressing these common complaints without prescribed drugs, not only do we feel better, but our relationships have the potential to improve dramatically.

Ultimately the cause of all our common complaints is higher stress levels. Researchers around the world all agree that chronic stress levels in our bodies provide a basis for any and all disease to take hold. An easy and quick solution for lowering our stress reactions is specific nutritional support combined with gender-smart relationship skills. Extra nutritional support is needed because stress depletes the body very quickly of essential nutrients. When a car engine is running more quickly, it uses fuel more quickly. When we are stressed, we need both extra nutrients and extra emotional support. Understanding what we need to take and where to get it requires education. Every week day at www.MarsVenus.com I have a live daily show where I freely answer questions and provide this much-needed new gender-specific insight.

At www.MarsVenus.com, we are happy to share what we have learned for creating healthy bodies and positive relationships. You can find a host of natural solutions for common complaints and feel confident that you have the power to feel fully alive with an abundance of energy and positive feelings that will enrich all your relationships.

You Set Your Own Appraisal

DR. SOBIA YAQUB

In its early years, plastic surgery was a miracle, a way to correct everything that you might have seen as an imperfection in your appearance. Yet, a funny thing began to manifest as plastic surgery became more widely available. People were never satisfied. For every fix, they saw another imperfection that needed to be corrected. Beautiful individuals were putting themselves under the knife, because they wanted to attain a level of perfection that was impossible.

What was the problem? Surprisingly enough, it had nothing to do with their physical bodies at all. It was their viewpoint and perspective. It was because they were giving all their power to other people and putting more value in other people's perception and opinion than their own opinion of themselves.

They were so focused on their outside that they ignored the issues and lack of confidence they had about who they were as individuals. They ignored the internal dialogue that kept manifesting in feelings of not being good enough, not being beautiful enough, and simply just not being enough.

"Whatever the mind can conceive and believe, the mind can achieve."
– Napoleon Hill

If you struggle in this area, I want you to understand that you can make a change. It starts with recognizing that your outside is a reflection of what you are focusing on inside. Once you change how you speak to yourself, then you will be able to accept and love yourself inside and out. I mean you have to redefine your self-image, which is independent of the opinions of others. That means getting to know your authentic self, not what was or is expected of you by others but what you truly, deep down from the bottom of your heart, expect from yourself. You do this by eliminating all kinds of fear, including fear of rejection, fear of disapproval, and fear of humiliation. If we look at history, the people who received the most approval from the world were the ones who were crystal clear about who they were and what they stood for, completely independent of others' opinions or perceptions about them. You can never reach your full potential unless you have healthy self-esteem.

I want you to imagine yourself in your car in New York City and amidst heavy traffic, trying to reach your desired destination by following your GPS. It is supposed to take you to the desired location, but keeps redirecting you again and again, taking you back home. It is extremely frustrating. Can you imagine saying to yourself: "Why is this GPS taking me home, which is far away from where I want to go?" It's because when you started your journey, you accidently selected home as your destination.

Similarly, when we were little, long before we started navigating our journey in this life, we formed a concept of ourselves, our abilities and expectations from ourselves and the world, which is called self-esteem or self-image. It is formed through our childhood experiences and our interpretation of those experiences, mainly with the authority figures in our lives, and somewhat by our peers and other people we interact with.

This concept of "self-esteem" serves as the destination of GPS. I believe by the time we are 7 years old, we have an almost complete concept of how the world is, who we are, and what space we occupy in relation to the world and the people around us. All our life, we behave and make decisions based upon that concept, unless it is fine-tuned by any significant life-altering event. Now imagine if that self-image was faulty and wrong as it was formed mainly through the years when we did not have a conscious or logical mind, and it was under control of the circumstances and people around us.

This means that our self-image and self-esteem, which is shaping our destiny each moment by the way we think, feel, act and react, depends on the intellect of the people around us as we were growing up, based on their limited perception about us as a child. Can you imagine that the most important factor which governs literally everything in our life has been formed without our informed consent?

This self-esteem or self-image was formed when we did not have insight about our true worth and is based on what we believed about ourselves as a child. If we were unfortunate enough to develop low self-esteem, then unless we fix our faulty self-esteem by reinterpreting the past experiences and making new sense of ourselves and the world, we cannot reach our goals and desires that are not congruent with our self-esteem.

IT STARTS WITH RECOGNIZING YOUR OWN VALUE

Self-image or self-esteem is defined as one's concept of oneself or of one's role and worth in this world. When you take the power back to redefine yourself and your true worth, you are putting yourself in the driver's seat to have the life that you deserve.

We all deserve to have wonderful things happen, to enjoy amazing experiences, to raise our families with values and beliefs that we cherish, and to find peace as we grow and learn throughout our journeys. Too often, however, we end up tripping ourselves up, because we focus on what we don't have, what isn't working, and allow our grief about what we have lost to keep us from seeing all that we have gained.

A key filtering system in our brain, which acts in congruence with our self-esteem and goals, is the Reticular Activating System (RAS). It serves as our slave. It is a network of neurons, which are located in the brain stem. It filters billions of bits of data and information, filters in the information that is important for us or that can serve us based on its alignment with our self-esteem. Have you ever noticed that when you decide you want to buy a car, say a Honda Accord, that you start seeing them everywhere?

It is as if, in the moment you decide on that vehicle, your RAS is activated. All of a sudden, Honda Accords, which were not within your awareness before, suddenly come into your awareness. In fact, you can count on your fingers how many Honda Accords passed you on the road that day.

Similarly, when you have a certain level of self-esteem or a certain self-image impressed upon your mind, your RAS will filter in the people, conditions, and opportunities that will help you achieve a life or goals congruent with your self-image. There is a term in the field of psychology named "Cognitive Dissonance," which is an uncomfortable state of mind when there are two or more inconsistent thoughts and beliefs. When you create a higher self-image, you create that dissonance between your old ways of being, thinking, feeling, communicating, and other habits that are not in sync with the new image. Your mind will then reject your old ways, thus propelling you to act in accordance with your new elevated self-esteem and self-image.

Throughout this chapter, I am focusing on how you can achieve a better life for yourself by creating a different mental picture of yourself. No matter who you are, you have a mental picture of yourself. Society also has an impact on molding your self-image. There are those expectations that you feel compelled to meet, and there is a guilt that seems to be built into all of us when we don't achieve those expectations.

Going through my own battle with low self-esteem, and after helping thousands of people conquer their low self-esteem, now your battle is my battle, as I know exactly who our enemy is and how we can kill that enemy. In other words, I can find out quite easily whether you have low self-esteem, which is holding you back from achieving your goals and dreams in any area of your life, what factors caused your faulty self-esteem, and how to fix it. Low self-esteem can be the root cause of obesity, failure in shedding those extra pounds, disturbed relationships, broken marriages, domestic violence, poor grades in school, issues with lack of money, failure in business, fear of speaking, social anxiety, compliance with medications, and in literally any area of life where you are struggling. I bet there is low self-esteem hiding there in your mind's GPS as your set destination, causing you to fail and come back to the same place over and over again.

Amidst all these factors, it can be easy to focus on the negative when it comes to your self-image and self-worth. It can be easy to look for quick fixes, instead of looking at the reasons why you feel a certain way about yourself. Fixing the outside is not going to fix the inside. Instead, you have to decide what you deserve and then focus on achieving that.

I was blessed to be born and raised in an amazing family with really high academic standards and a strong discipline. My mother and father are the most supportive parents I have seen, who invested so much time and energy to make us independent and successful human beings. We had servants, chefs and a chauffeur at our disposal all the time. All we were expected to do was to study and get good grades. My father served in the military as a commando. He was passionate about his duty. He fought in two wars. He was the best athlete of his time in the army, and he participated and represented our country in the world's military championship in Athens, Greece. He attributes this to his unshakeable belief in himself and his abilities, and of course the help of God.

My mom is an amazing lady. She is the most hard-working woman I have ever seen, with extraordinary resolve and perseverance. She had very high expectations for her children's education, and a vision for our performance in the world, and she was and still is very much involved in our lives. With an academically challenging environment at home, my oldest brother grew up to be a civil engineer and the rest of us, four siblings, became medical doctors. As the youngest, I was treated as the "baby of the house." I was pampered, spoon-fed, and guided in every step. My siblings were all exceptionally good in studies, and particularly in science and math, which were not my strengths. I was an artist and I had a passion for fine arts. Literally all my school books were full of pictures of faces and cartoons that I drew.

I used to represent my school in fine arts competitions, but somehow, I developed low self-esteem because I was constantly gauging myself based upon understanding of concepts of math and science. I overlooked my strengths. I was comparing my weaknesses with my siblings' strengths.

My friends in childhood were a reflection of my low self-esteem, as I made friends with the kids who were the "back benchers." I was associating myself with the low achievers. My group of friends and I were the ones who would never listen to the lectures and made fun of the teachers. To the utter surprise of others, I would get really good results at the end of the year because I learnt some techniques to accelerate my comprehension and retention. My focus would be as sharp as a laser and I would lock myself in a room with a set of goals and deadlines that I resolved to achieve, in order to keep up with my siblings. Of course, my friends used to get jealous of me because they believed I did not deserve to get better grades than them.

I was a shy kid, but I was genuinely interested in people and always wanted to help them. That was a reason I bought into my mother's vision of me becoming a doctor.

While my older brothers and sisters managed to have a huge library with books in alphabetical order on the shelves, I would seldom read a single book. Still, I managed to write my own book of poems, and create my little magazines every few months with pictures cut from different magazines, containing my own observations about different actors and TV programs. I started all that when I was 8 years old. Our friends, and guests to our home, were amused to see my funny magazines and my poems. My sister used to tell me I was very observant and creative. I spent most of my day in my room with my dolls, painting or writing, because I was not comfortable among people as I was shy.

The education system in Pakistan is very different from the American system. We have two major exams. The first is at the end of 10th grade, which determines whether you will go into Pre-Med, and one at 12th grade, which determines whether you will get admission in the medical school.

Some moments in your life can make a drastic change in the course of your life. I remember that one day of my school vividly. I was in 10th grade and it was the last quarter of the year. I was, as usual, sitting in the very back row with my "not so motivated" friends, not paying attention to the teacher and drawing my friend's face on my book. Our math teacher, who was no less than terror for the class, caught me. She knew my whole family and had taught my two older sisters. She called me to the front and asked me to solve the problem on the blackboard. I had no clue at first, since I had not been listening and, second, math was never my strength. I could not solve the problem. She gave me a stern look and in front of the whole class said, "Sobia, this was such a simple problem and you failed to solve it. The board exams are around the corner. All of your brothers and sisters excelled in studies and I am certain that won't be able to keep up with the image of your family and you can never become a doctor, as you waste your time drawing and painting."

That day, I felt very discouraged, because there were only three months left for our major exam. I was very sensitive to others' opinions and assessments of me because I valued others' opinions of me more than my own opinion. I went home feeling rejected.

My dad saw me and he was very in tune with our moods, so he asked me: "Sobia, are you okay?" I told him, "Papa, I feel like I will not be able to fulfill your expectations and I will not score well in my exams." I explained what Mrs. K said, and I never forgot what he said that day. "Sobia, you are the most brilliant girl I have ever seen. She can only see the tip of the iceberg. You and only you know about your true potential. Please don't let her faulty perception of you discourage you. Remember in this world, you set your own appraisal."

Those words stuck in my mind. You set your own appraisal. That means all what the world gives back to you is a reflection of your own self-esteem. My dad then went to our library, took out a very tiny book and handed it to me. The book was called Psycho-Cybernetics, written by a plastic surgeon Maxwell Maltz, which describes the self-image and how to use visualization to change your self-image.

Since I am a right brain dominant person and I used to daydream a lot, practicing these visualizations was a piece of cake for me. In fact, I enjoyed the visualization techniques so much that I practiced them almost an hour a day. I visualized myself doing great in all my subjects, including math. I redefined my self-image. I visualized my name on the honor board of my school where each year the name of the student who stood first in the whole school is written. These visualizations and positive frame of mind gave me the energy to study day and night.

These visualizations and positive frame of mind gave me the energy to study day and night. As part of my visualizations, I created a vision board, which I divided into three sections. In the middle section, I created a painting of myself holding an award stating "Sobia Yaqub, 1st position, Azam Garrison School." On one side of the board, I created an hourly timetable for the next 3 months, outlining the steps to achieving my goal. On the final section, I wrote a poem. Each section contributed to my larger goal of achieving a place on that honor board.

"Yes, I am a loving and creative soul,
I am an artist who is driven by my passion.
And by the Grace of God, I will become a doctor by profession.
And with my knowledge I will help people,
as elevating others is my obsession."
– Dr. Sobia Yaqub

I wanted to prove to my math teacher that she was wrong in her perception of me and at the same time I wanted to make my parents proud of me.

"The best revenge is massive success."
– Frank Sinatra

Finally, I took my exams. The results came in and I stood first in the whole school, among about 150 girls in the 10th grade. My name and picture were published in the newspaper. I got into the best college in Pakistan, Kinnard college, and then went to the medical school I dreamt of. It was the same medical school my sisters graduated from. I became a firm believer in the power of visualization. I met Mrs. K in the school in the principal's office, where she told me, "Sobia, we are proud of you."

It all happened because I didn't believe in her limited perception of me. I believed in my own vision and my God-given abilities. I valued my own assessment of myself more than how she assessed me.

Do you find yourself bound by cultural expectations? Have you allowed those expectations to impact how you perceive yourself? Cultural expectations have a way of hemming us in, giving us a reason to judge ourselves harshly, often without real cause. When you explore your passions and find the things that bring you joy, that might not meet the expectations of your culture or society as a whole.

Per Dr. Wayne Dyer, the people who get the most approval from the world are the people who need others' approval the least. It is very important to understand the concept. A person with good self-esteem does not need approval from other people, as his own approval is enough for him. It is similar to a person who leaves home after having a heavy breakfast. He isn't looking for restaurants to go eat at because he is already full.

Let's look at how you describe yourself to others. What qualities do you think of first? Are they negative ones, or do you focus on your positive attributes first? It can be easy to slip into a negative state of mind, focusing on the things you need to improve or the areas in which you feel you fall short.

Self-esteem, in simple terms, is basically about how you see yourself, what you expect from yourself that dictates how you carry yourself in this world, and ultimately has indirect control on how others treat you and how you take advantage of your circumstances, rather than allowing circumstances and people to take advantage of you.

I got married, and soon after, I landed in New York in January 2001. My husband and I lived in Manhattan. I came across many individuals who would tell me that they couldn't understand my foreign accent. Had I not believed in myself and carried a healthy self-esteem, I would never have been chosen as a physician coach by my organization. Part of my position included coaching other physicians in different primary care settings.

Can you believe it? I have been coaching the physicians who were born and raised in the United States, helping them to learn how to communicate with the American patients on a one-to-one level. On top of that, I was getting paid for my coaching services. I had to use my visualization practices to overcome many hurdles in my life, but I have also enjoyed many opportunities as a result.

When I was recognized as the "The Women of the Year 2017," I took my parents with me to the pride of performance award ceremony in Anaheim, California. They were called on stage as well. When we came down after receiving the award, my mom said, "Sobia , I am proud of you. You pursued your passions along with your career, and today you were recognized for helping others with your God-gifted passions."

I believe all of us have a calling and a purpose hidden deep inside, and only we can discover what our calling is. I auction my art work and all the profits go to my nonprofit charitable organization. It gives me fulfillment. We need to find ways to fulfill our souls.

I am not advocating for you to have an inflated sense of yourself, to the point that you can't see areas where you need to improve or want to better yourself. Instead, I want you to avoid the other extreme, where you are so hard on yourself that it is mentally and emotionally damaging. When you reach that point, you can't help yourself or others. You end up shortchanging the world because deny your gifts, talents, and abilities, and you don't allow your unique contribution to be felt.

Think of all the ways that you talk to yourself on a daily basis; the mental dialogue that you have and the points you choose to focus on. When you are presented with negative situations or less than ideal circumstances, do you see them as an opportunity for growth or do you see them as another reason to be down on yourself? Focusing on how you are not meeting specific expectations can be a key to bringing yourself down and creating an internal dialogue that damages you.

When you get into a negative loop, you are devaluing yourself. You are choosing to define yourself as damaged goods of little value. Others may see your value and be frustrated at why you don't see it as well. They are not privy to all the thoughts in your head, the ones that focus on all the ways you don't measure up. It can be hard to find your value with that type of dialogue on constant repeat.

Still, I want you to start the process of changing that inner dialogue by focusing on replacing one negative thought with a positive one. For instance, if you are focusing on some aspects of your appearance that you don't like and wish you could improve, then find one part of your physical appearance that you are proud of and focus on that. Internally, you need to remind yourself about those unique aspects of yourself that are your contributions to the world. Be thankful for them.

Be mindful of how you talk to yourself about who you are. Negative thinking can become so pervasive that you don't even realize that you are doing it. Instead, that negative internal dialogue becomes a record that is stuck in one groove, never moving forward. Being mindful means consciously taking the time to examine what you are telling yourself, and making changes based on those assessments.

Time and again, you will find that when you consciously focus on that internal dialogue, you can start to pick up on those negative trains of thought that are limiting you and causing damage to how you view yourself.

I will be talking about being mindful throughout these pages, because I want you to recognize that too many things you tell yourself are there because you created an unconscious habit. You will have to be mindfully aware, in order to change that habit and create a new one to take its place. Your mindset needs to shift from the negative to the positive, and that starts by recognizing your value and then focusing on how your value is a gift to the world.

CHANGING THE DIALOGUE MEANS CHANGING YOUR MINDSET

I find that the first thing I have to recognize is that I do have value. Not just as a spouse, daughter, and mother, but as an individual. The world is richer because I am alive in it, and the world is richer because of you as well. Each of us has value, and brings a special talent, a unique gift with us as our contribution to making the world a better place.

When you talk to yourself, focus on what you can offer to others, not what you can't. Focusing on the negative without a clear plan to address it is a sure way to bring down your sense of self and create a mindset of complaining, negativity, and hopelessness.

Part of what can help you to change that mindset is to make a conscious effort each day to focus on a positive aspect of your life, and who you are as an individual. The reason that this is so critical is that every day you are being bombarded with the negative. It is on the news, on television, and on the radio. Social media is full of information that focuses on how you don't measure up.

When you make a conscious effort to focus on a positive in your life, you are shifting the internal dialogue away from the negative. Start with a mantra on a daily basis. It could be a mantra of something that you are thankful for. Every day you need to think of something different. Don't just start the day by saying you are thankful for the same thing over and over. Then it becomes something you do by rote and it does not carry the same value over time.

Instead, choose to be mindful about the things that you appreciate in your life. It could be a gift of patience, or the ability to help others through food, music, or a listening ear. You might be thankful for the ability to work and provide for yourself and your family. No matter what you choose to be thankful for, be in the moment and give meaningful thanks for that gift, ability, or circumstance.

Even if you are going through a difficult period in your life, find a reason to be thankful. When you are grieving the loss of a loved one, it can be hard to find that reason to be thankful. But it is there in the memories you have.

You clearly are thankful for the moments that you can look back on, that can make you smile.

My point is not that you will not have painful circumstances in your life, but that you need to look beyond the moment to find the reason for thankfulness, or to find how you can benefit from those circumstances.

I know that during my immigration to the U.S., I had to find reasons for joy and thankfulness, even as my world was shifting. The culture was different, how individuals viewed the world was different, and I had to adapt. I had to recognize that my gift was empathy and the ability to see a person, not just as a body to be healed, but as a person who needed my knowledge and skill to mend their mind, body, and spirit. It gave me a unique perspective, one that others valued, and resulted in my assignment to train other doctors on how to deal with patients.

As a doctor, I have to think of the whole person, not just one part or another. When you are talking about your own value, you need to see all of your value, not just one or two things. It is not about focusing on a few nuggets but seeing all the amazing facets of who you are.

I believe that it is critical to have empathy for others, recognizing that they may be dealing with the difficult parts of their own journey. At the same time, however, you need to have empathy for yourself. You might be willing to give someone else a pass because they are grieving a loss, but you don't do the same for yourself. If you get nothing else from this chapter, I want you to hear this: Be kind to yourself!

Part of improving your self-image involves not only focusing on areas of your life where you can be grateful but concentrating on the positive aspects of your life. There are going to be things that you wish you could change or that you want to be different, but the reality is that you do not need to dwell on them to the point that they bring you down to a level of seeing yourself as less than.

START WITH VISUALIZATION

You can start to improve your self-image by using a tool known as visualization. It is important to realize that your mind has powerful abilities to create and shift your reality. When you make a conscious effort to visualize a different path for yourself, and you do so on a daily basis, you will start to see circumstances shift in your daily life.

Let's think about this in terms of cars. If you are interested in purchasing a new car, you might do research on a specific model or various bells and whistles. Then you might begin to notice those types of cars are everywhere. Did that car really become more popular, or are you more aware of it now because you are interested in purchasing one?

The point here is that what you dwell on mentally becomes part of your reality. If you want to change how you view yourself, then you need to dwell on the positive aspects of your personality, on your goals, and on what you offer to others. As you make a conscious effort to visualize these things, then you will find it easier to acknowledge them in your reality.

The benefits of visualization are vast. Visualization can help you to accelerate your goals and dreams, simply because it gives you a means to be hyper-focused, and confident in your ability to achieve your goals. Using visualization, you can stimulate your creative side, allowing yourself to come up with creative methods to achieve your goals. Too often, individuals find themselves stuck, because they have a goal but no clear way to achieve it.

Creative thinking takes you out of the box, but also gives you the means to come up with ideas or methods that might not have occurred to you before.

Part of visualization involves reprogramming your brain, helping you to recognize resources that can assist you. Like the car, once you are focused on something, your subconscious will draw your attention to resources that you might not have noticed before. I find that it is easier to find what you need when you are focused on it and your brain is giving it top priority. Visualization is a way for you to put order to your brain's input, helping your conscious and subconscious mind to recognize the priorities and then bring them to your attention.

At this point, any discussion of visualization would be meaningless if I did not discuss the law of attraction. Simply put, the law of attraction is one of the most powerful laws in the universe. You attract into your life what you focus on. Whatever you give your time, energy, and attention to will then be attracted into your life. If you are positive and focused on things that give you joy and excitement, you will draw more of those things into your life.

The same is true of negative energy. When you send it out, you are going to receive it back. Now let's apply this to your self-image. If you are focused on the negative aspects of your self-image, you will see more of them. You are attracting that negativity. However, if you decide to focus on the positive aspects of your self-image, you will draw more of those positives into your life.

According to Jack Canfield, "The Law of Attraction allows for infinite possibilities, infinite abundance, and infinite joy. It knows no order of difficulty, and it can change your life in every way."

When you choose to think differently about situations, when you choose what to focus on, and when you choose to respond differently, you will draw different experiences and responses in return. You have the ability to choose your future, to participate in creating the life you want. It all starts by visualizing it, and training your brain to work in harmony with those visualizations.

Notice that the point is to ask for and focus on what you want, not what you don't want. Shifting your focus through visualization is key to having the impact you want through the Law of Attraction.

Finally, visualization is going to help you get excited about achieving your goals and objectives. You are motivating yourself to achieve your dreams and to build the life that you want, one that gives you purpose and allows you to leave a legacy for others.

Here are a few visualization techniques that you can put into practice in your life. Once you start making a habit of them, you will be able to benefit more fully from the effects.

• Start by making it a daily practice. Those who attain the most with visualization start by taking a few minutes each day to rehearse what they want to accomplish. Doing so daily keeps it fresh in your mind and creates that hyper-focus you need to achieve it.

• Give it detail. Part of the effectiveness of visualization is that you are creating a detailed image that your brain can focus on making your reality. To make it more real, you need to focus on sharpening every aspect of your goal. Imagine your clothing, your facial expressions, the colors, sounds, and even how things might feel. Include your own feelings, to give the visualization real depth.

• Put yourself into that moment and infuse it throughout your body. Give yourself complete power to touch, smell, taste, see, and hear. The more real it is in your visualization, the more your brain will want to make it your reality.

Throughout these points, I was essentially teaching you about the power of creation that you have. In fact, we all have this ability, but so few of us take the time to use it effectively. Negative self-image can play a big part in why individuals are not using their powers of creation effectively. Instead, they focus on what is not going right and as a result, they draw more of the same into their lives.

Let's shift this discussion to your self-image. Are you always focusing on what you do wrong, on the ways that you "fail" at what you try to do? I am not talking about healthy self-analysis, where you look at your actions with an eye on continuous improvement. I am talking about beating yourself up for how you reacted, how you behaved, or how you didn't achieve as much as you had hoped. When you focus strictly on the negative, you are going to find yourself making more mistakes and drawing more of that negativity into your life.

Have you ever had a really bad day? We all have. As the day goes along, the more you focus on what has already gone wrong, the more that seems to go wrong. It becomes a vicious cycle, one that can be hard to break. However, with a conscious effort, you can break that cycle. Now think of your life in the large sense. You have the capability to break the cycle of negativity in your life and create something different.

To make your visualization even more powerful, use pictures of yourself accomplishing your goal. Doing so can help you give that detail to your visualizations that can help you to truly see it. No matter what goal you have in your life, be it financial, career, recreation, or experiences you want to have, visualization can be critical to successfully bringing it to fruition.

To support your visualizations, it is important to use affirmations. They are helpful in reinforcement, because they evoke not only the picture of what you want, but also the experience of already having what you want. When you repeat an affirmation several times a day, it strengthens your motivation and programs your subconscious to do whatever it takes to make that goal or objective a reality.

As you can see, using visualizations and affirmations enable you to change your beliefs, assumptions, and opinions. Harness your brain to create the results you want, and harness your ability into a purposeful direction.

Make sure that your visualizations and affirmations are part of your daily routine. It is best to do them mornings and evenings. However, you don't want to spend the whole day thinking only of your goals, because then you won't be able to enjoy the moment. You may find that you are more willing to take chances and seize opportunities when you have a regular routine of visualization and affirmations. Daily routines can help you to stay balanced and allow you to appreciate the life that you have right now, as well as work towards the one you want to have in the future.

Your mental focus will shift to what you want to achieve, and you will have less time to focus on any negativity that may filter into your life from time to time by circumstances out of your control.

ACT WITH YOUR CIRCUMSTANCES

Throughout your life, you are going to be presented with circumstances that are beyond your control. The loss of a loved one, unexpected natural disasters, or even a sudden illness can all negatively impact your life. However, you can choose your reaction, and how those circumstances impact you.

Our self-esteem is conveyed consciously, and largely unconsciously, through subliminal stimuli. Based on studies, 95% of our brain activity is beyond our awareness, and that is where our self-esteem lies. Only 5% of our brain activity is conscious. The way we stand, the way we sit, the way we talk, the way we breathe, the tone of voice and the words we choose, the way we make eye contact, and the way we shake hands are all dictated by our self-esteem, and all of them teach people how to treat us. Our conscious and unconscious thoughts are in constant communication with the universe.

Not that you won't have an emotional response, but you can choose to take that emotional response and channel it towards your benefit. I find that every difficult circumstance presents me with an opportunity to bring my best self to the table. I can take it and use it as a learning opportunity, instead of a reason to stop trying to achieve in my life or move forward.

Your thoughts trigger emotions, and your emotions are often the trigger for your actions. When you take a moment to consciously control your thoughts about a situation or circumstance, you are taking control of your emotions and, thereby, your actions. Remember too, that when you choose your reaction, you are choosing what you want to focus on and are giving the Law of Attraction the information that it needs to bring things into your life.

Most of this will start with shifting your vibrations. What do I mean by this? It means that you need to focus on creating positive emotions in the world, including joy, love, peace, and appreciation. When you practice feeling these emotions, and creating these emotions with your thoughts, you are going to change your vibration.

Once you do that, you will start to notice that your reality begins to match that positive vibration. You will draw to yourself more of what you are putting out in terms of positive energy. Granted, you might not feel joy every day.

However, it is important to stop negative emotions in their tracks. If you aren't feeling joyful, then visualize circumstances where you did feel joyful and bring that feeling into the moment.

Many individuals focus on what they don't want, and then wonder why they are not achieving everything that they imagine is possible for their lives. The reason is that the Law of Attraction is going to bring what you focus on, either positive or negative. Therefore, it is key to focus on what you want to achieve and then act to back it up. When you do so, you allow your unique contribution to benefit yourself and others.

At this moment, I want to shift the discussion away from how you benefit from the Law of Attraction and instead focus on how you can use it to help others.

I have spent a lot of time talking about the importance of positive thinking, bringing positive energy into your life by choosing what to focus on, and I have given you some techniques to help you bring your thoughts and actions in line with what you want to achieve. Now I want to talk about how you can use that to help others.

Remember, you can't choose your circumstances, but you can choose how to react to them. Your example can be an inspiration to others who are looking for a way to deal with their own challenging circumstances. When they see how you handle your challenges, they are likely to want to gain a deeper understanding of what you are doing to achieve your results.

The treatment of low or faulty self-esteem incorporates a wide variety of methods and techniques, including visualization, neuro-linguistic programming (NLP), hypnosis, and psychology, and the treatment varies based on each individual. Some individuals may even need pharmaceutical intervention to temporarily address symptoms of anxiety that may arise as my patients embark on a new journey of behaving in a certain way.

THE BENEFITS OF MENTORING

Serving as a mentor for someone can help them to gain knowledge and experiences that they might otherwise have missed. Your legacy can often be wrapped up in what you do for others, how you help them to achieve their own goals, how you inspire them to think creatively about their situation, and how you give them something to reach for in their lives.

Success tends to breed a better sense of self-image, because positive experiences feed positive thinking, which draws more positive experiences your way. That positive self-image is reflected in how you treat others and will impact how they react to you. What you put out into the universe comes back to you.

All of us have a purpose, one that allows us to have a positive impact on others. Your self-image is going to impact how much you are able to assist others, inspire them, or provide mentorship. You have the capability to build more than you have ever imagined possible, and it starts by focusing on what you want to build and then acting in accordance with your vision.

What gets you excited to get up in the morning? Think of all the different activities or events that bring you joy as you participate in them. Are there ways that you are able to dignify others by your actions? I often think of the proverb, "There is more happiness in giving than in receiving." The reason I want to bring this up is because when you help others, it positively impacts your own self-image.

When you feel your self-image improving, it motivates you to step outside of your comfort zone. Perhaps you have an idea for a business that will solve a problem in your community, while providing sustainable jobs for individuals looking for work. When you are in a negative vein of thinking, your actions reflect that negativity, and you will talk yourself out of pursuing that idea.

Yet, when you shift your internal dialogue, suddenly, you are able to see how your idea could work and you see any obstacles as challenges instead of roadblocks. My point is that your self-image can either block you from moving forward, or it can be the catalyst that starts you on a path to achieving your purpose and impacting others.

At this point, I want to focus on a simple principle that is critical to your success. Whatever you think about, whatever you make your focus, is what you will bring into your life. Acknowledging this fact can help you to recognize your own power to create and help you to work in harmony with that power to achieve your life purpose.

As part of that effort, I want you to look for a mentor, one who can help you to think outside the box and hold you accountable when you are allowing negative thinking to dominate. When I work with individuals, I help them to see how critical their own internal dialogue is to their success. When I speak to myself with an empathic voice, truly recognize my legitimate concerns, and then work to address them, I see myself reaching the goals and dreams that I set for myself.

I want to help you to achieve that as well. Your vision is unique to you, and the world needs that unique vision. We can all sit down and create a laundry list of items that need to be fixed or changed in the world. Complaining about it rarely results in true change, but just leads to more negative energy. I want to spark a change in you, one that can help us all to shift the energy from negative to positive.

As part of your visualization and affirmations, it is important to recognize that what you are creating in your own reality has ripple effects across a much larger pond. Circling back to how your actions can impact others, you need to recognize that the energy you use to create your reality will help you to inspire or bring down others. The choice is truly up to you.

Everything that you do when it comes to creating positive energy in your life is going to take practice. You aren't going to wake up one day with a brand-new self-image and a completely different way of talking to yourself. Instead, you are going to have to make a conscious decision and then keep practicing on a daily basis.

I am a firm believer that you get what you expect out of life, with the help of God. This is my passion, to help you live your life at your peak potential. This can only happen if you redefine your self-esteem and let go of the wrong labels that were put on you by ignorant people. Don't let anyone else design your life. Only you have the right to estimate your worth. The only way to get to where you want to go is to have the insight of where you are, and to redefine your self-image and change your internal representation. Otherwise, it is like navigating the world with the wrong map in your hands.

As you practice, you are creating new patterns of thinking, and new habits. Your brain will learn and, eventually, a positive frame of mind and self-image will become the norm. It will be your default position. I look forward to helping you achieve the self-image that allows you to benefit others with your unique contribution, while allowing you to achieve your life's purpose!

For more information about Dr. Sobia Yaqub, please go to www.Doctoryslifecoaching.com or you can call Dr. Sobia directly at 972-325-8205.

How To Do I.O.A.L.

A Simple Financial Blueprint

BERNARD H. DALZIEL

T he tried and true principles of saving and spending less seem to be the only financial literacy that most of us are exposed to. For so many of us, that means we are armed with little knowledge about one of the most important aspects of our lives, which is how to manage the money that we all need to function and enjoy the experiences that give meaning and depth to our lives.

Throughout this chapter, I am going to share the I.O.A.L. system, one that focuses on four key areas that are critical to building your wealth and helping you grow your net worth. Along the way, I am going to help you gain a better understanding of how to meet your financial goals and positively impact your future. Let's get started!

THE BEGINNING OF MY FINANCIAL EDUCATION

I love to help others help themselves by providing solutions that can help them double their income and triple their time off. When I started out, it wasn't easy for me. I had a hard time growing up. I was definitely considered a problem child. In fact, I probably spent more time in the hallway than I did in the classroom!

Yet, that was not time that I wasted. Instead, I used it to dream and stretch my imagination, growing and developing my EQ versus my IQ. Since I was out there already, I got to know everyone. To me, a stranger was just a friend that I hadn't met yet.

I was ready to quit school at age 12. Yet, there were moments and individuals that helped me during this academic struggle. I had a counselor who taught me a secret that helped me to learn the 9 multiplication tables in seventh grade. At that point, I was skipping school on a regular basis. I was hauled back to school by a truant officer and assigned to a counselor named Tom. He became my friend, and told me that if I was determined to leave school, there were certain basic things that I needed to know, such as reading, writing, and arithmetic.

That was when he found out that I didn't even know my 9 multiplication tables. He helped me fill out a job application with a short quiz on it. One part of the quiz was the 9 multiplication tables. I had to write the multiplication table from 1 to 9, put four triangles in a square, and then mail it in. As I did the multiplication table, I counted down (see the diagram). Then I put an X in the box. Now I decided to mail it myself, but being dyslexic, I wrote my name and address on the front, and the address I wanted to send it to on the back. I forgot to put a stamp on it, but I did remember to put it in the mailbox. A week later, I received the call to come in for an interview for the position of an office boy. More about that later.

Notice all the things I did wrong, yet how it all came together. By putting the address in the wrong spot, but forgetting the stamp, the letter was essentially returned to the place that I wanted it to go all along.

I also read the book Psycho-Cybernetics by Maxwell Maltz. He was a plastic surgeon who found that individuals were no happier after plastic surgery, simply because they had changed their outside, but not their inside, which included how they thought about themselves.

I made the decision to change how I viewed myself. No longer was I going to see myself as an academic failure, but as someone with unique gifts and talents that I could share with others. I decided to dedicate my life to helping others to help themselves by providing easy to understand information. One area in particular that I knew I could help was by creating a simple formula that gives people a way to create a written financial plan or blueprint. It was meant to help them change the way they think about their finances and give them an easy step-by-step process for financial freedom and independence.

If the elevator for success no longer works for you, then I want you to have the ability to take the stairs, one step at a time. Most people don't plan to fail, they just fail to plan.

Granted, I still had obstacles and challenges to face. I was dyslexic, which made school a trial, as I mentioned earlier. Then I started down a self-destructive path, one that led to alcohol, smoking, and drugs. It was a way of life that could have cost me mine. Still determined to follow this path of self-destruction, I lost my father at the age of 15. Now, I had to stop doing drugs because I had to step up and help my mother. It was time for me to grow up.

My mother, Irene Richardson, is an impressive individual, one who raised her children with a sense of purpose and a desire to learn. Even to this day, she is active, and her routine could wear me out! She taught me that common sense is not that common these days. At the ripe age of 89 years old, she takes no pills, just nutritional supplements, and leads a water aerobics class 6 days a week. Her one day off is for God, and she knows that God answers all who take a knee.

As I got closer to 16, I realized that I needed to be a man. I stopped using drugs and got my driver's license. I also joined the swim team. I truly started to take control of my life and shape it to fit my vision, instead of allowing others' opinions of my capabilities define me. By 19, I had taken the exam for industrial first aid, and I became a first aid attendant and night watchman.

Then I took on an apprenticeship and became a distribution engineer in Vancouver. At that time, I was making $50,000 a year. It was a chance to party, and I did that until I was 37. That was when I met my mentor Raymond Aaron, through his Dr. Al Lowry course on investing in real estate. I also took a Thurston Wright course. My world was on a high. I cleaned myself up, mind, body, and soul. I took a year off to work on my personal relationship with my daughter. At the time, I was earning $5,000 a month.

That was when life threw up a huge obstacle. My marriage was ending. The divorce was difficult, draining me mentally, physically, emotionally, and especially financially. Suddenly a judge was telling me that half my monthly income ($2,500) needed to go to my soon-to-be ex-wife. I was in debt and going through the divorce from hell when I reconnected with Raymond Aaron.

I signed up for his monthly mentoring program using my credit card. I was adding more debt, but Raymond told me to give him two years and I would be able to change my life. I completed the mentoring program and I still have the certificate hanging on my wall. I completed my divorce and refinanced my debts to a comfortable level.

The next few years saw my life taking an amazing turn for the better. I met and married the love of my life and was able to help her raise her son and godson. Both of these young men went on to receive Master's degrees in their chosen fields. My daughter became an RN and now I am about to be a grandfather. My life is rich and full of blessings, but I realized that now was the best time to reach out to others and share a way to make a financial blueprint simple. My goal is to make complicated things simple, and help us all to achieve a life of peace in the process.

One of the things I credit with helping me to achieve this level of success in my life is that I took advantage of having mentors. Too often, we assume that our experiences make us the best guide to create the future we want. I learned that this is not the case. Robert Kiyosaki, author of *Rich Dad, Poor Dad*, also served as a mentor for me. His cash flow game, and explanation of how and why we work, helped me to make changes in my mindset. I also found mentors in Brian Tracy; Fred Synder, a radio personality on *Of Your Money*; and Ralph Hahmann, author of *Pension Paradigm*.

Clearly, mentors helped me to define goals, create timelines, and stay accountable. I want you to find financial success, and that starts with tapping into the wisdom and experiences of others. If you would like to speak with me about mentoring, contact me at www.BenardHD.com.

WHAT IS A BLUEPRINT?

A blueprint is a planning tool or document created to guide you in the process of building or creating your financial success. It can include your priorities, projects, budgets, and future planning. It can be revised, but serves as a guide to help you understand where you are in your financial journey. You can also make adjustments or fine-tune it on a daily, weekly, monthly, quarterly, or yearly basis. This is because various factors in your life can change. My divorce was one such event, but I am sure that you can think of many other examples.

You could win the lottery and be a millionaire, or you could lose everything that you own to a natural disaster. Heaven forbid, you could get into a car accident and sustain severe injuries or, worse, lose a family member to death.

The point is that, whether you recognize it or not, we all have a financial blueprint, from the homeless man on the corner to the wealthiest CEO. It might be a conscious or unconscious thing, but it does exist. Others have it written down. What I am about to teach you can be written out by a 7th grader. Many of us don't have money problems per se but have accumulated a lot of debt and expenses.

I believe that if we learned this strategy in 7th grade, it could create a shift in how we handle our finances, allowing us to avoid the large amount of debt that most individuals carry today. What a difference we could create for the next generation by teaching them about saving and investment wealth accumulation, the difference between good and bad debt, and more. The point is that what you are doing now is based on what you were taught in the past. Yet, that is not going to help you to create the future that you want. The past doesn't equal the future.

HOW DO YOU CREATE A FINANCIAL BLUEPRINT?

Throughout this chapter, I am going to give you the tools to create your financial blueprint. I just want you to remember that you are trying to keep things simple, so don't be afraid of having to make adjustments along the way. As Raymond Aaron says, just keep failing forward. The important thing is to just do it!

You are starting on a journey, and you need to draw the map that will help you to reach your final destination. The phrase to do expresses motion or moving in a specific direction towards a person, place, or thing. The point is that you have to take action. Right now, you have to get out a pen and a piece of paper. I want you to get everything out of your head. Start with creating four quadrants, as seen in the diagram.

Next, I need you to collect information together, so you know how much debt you have and how much income you have, such as income statements, investment income, etc. When you do your first financial blueprint, I want you to go low on income and high on expenses. As you do the math, you will be able to see whether you are cash flowing positively or negatively.

Most broke people go high on income and low on expenses, then they wonder why they are part of the 80% of Americans struggling financially. Now that you are reading this chapter and committed to changing your financial future, you are on the way to creating meaningful change in your life.

The definition of do is to perform an act or duty, to execute a piece of work, to accomplish something, or to complete or finish it. I want you to see this financial blueprint as a means to complete the action of understanding your finances, so that you can make informed decisions now to create a different future.

It is up to you to do the work. I am merely here to provide guidance and inspiration as you follow the directions to complete your financial blueprint.

INCOME **I** **OWE** **O** N E T W E A L T H

Gross=

Net=

Min=

Target=

Outrageous=

$ [ ]

Accomodation=

Transportation=

Entertainment
& Communication=

Meal=

Spending=

Deductible=

Non/Deductible=

$ [ ]

ASSETS **A** **LIABILITIES** **L** N E T W O R T H

Value=

Minimum=

Target=

Outrageous=

$ [ ]

Financial=

Legal=

Deductible=

Non/Deductible=

$ [ ]

I OWE AL

My uncle Al gave me a simple way to do a financial blueprint formula. He explained that what goes in must go out. It is like breathing. The body must take in oxygen, in order to expel carbon dioxide. The concept is so automatic for us that, without even thinking, all of us take regular and consistent breaths throughout the day. Here is what is interesting, however. When we take the time to do conscious breathing, where we mindfully concentrate on how we breathe, suddenly the whole tone of our breathing becomes different.

You get more out of it, and your mindset shifts. You sharpen your focus and it proves to be beneficial to bringing peace to your mind and body. There are many different ways of creating this focus, a sharpness of the mind. I can think of several, including yoga, stretching, meditation, and more. The point is that you are creating an internal focus that can help you to achieve anything that you set your mind to.

The formula is I.O.A.L., Income (I), Out of Wealth (O), Assets (A), and Liabilities (L). Each of these areas is part of what you need in order to create wealth and grow your net worth. I am going to cover each of these areas and help you to understand this formula and how you can use it to benefit your financial plans.

INCOME (I)

What is income? Strictly speaking, it is the money that you bring in, either through your job or investments. Consider this the way that you breathe in,

71

drawing in the financial capital you need to pay for your lifestyle, including your basic needs and your wants. Another way to look at it is the money that an individual receives from a company in exchange for goods and services. You are exchanging your hours and skills for dollars. The reality is that your income is often capped by the number of hours you work in a day, the number of miles you can drive, or the number of customers you can serve.

Investing, on the other hand, brings in money but the exchange is not the same. The rich use money to invest and make more money, often while they are involved in other activities. Instead of exchanging their time and skills, they are providing capital, and that means their income truly can't be capped.

Most of us think of our income in terms of what we make in an hour, multiply it by the number of hours worked, and then do the math to come up with our annual income. Yet, the reality is that you don't make that much. The amount that you did all the math to come up with is just a gross number and doesn't reflect what you actually get to spend.

What you need to focus on instead is your net income. This income is essentially what you bring home after you pay taxes, health insurance, and any other deductions. You might find that, in the end, your annual salary based on your hourly wages is significantly higher than what you actually bring home on your paycheck. Why is this important to understand?

Simply put, many individuals make spending decisions based on what they make in gross income and then wonder why they are struggling to pay the bills or meet their financial goals. They are focused on the wrong number, and its negative impacts their ability to grow their net wealth. Let's start by determining what your net monthly income is. I want you to write down every source of income that you receive on a monthly basis before taxes and deductions. Once you have that number, you can then subtract your taxes and deductions to come up with your net monthly income.

Now that you know what that amount is, it is time to look at where that income goes. Remember, many individuals plan their expenses based on their gross income, which means that they are going to find themselves in the hole every month. How often do you find yourself struggling from paycheck to paycheck, barely getting by, let alone putting yourself in a position to save and invest?

I want you to understand that just by acknowledging that there is a difference between your gross and net income, you are already ahead of so many individuals who are exchanging hours and skills for dollars. This is because you see the potential to rid yourself of the cap that comes with exchanging hours for dollars, and see the possibilities to increase your income with no limits.

When you choose to invest, it needs to be from the head and not the heart. Too often, people fall for a great story, but a poor business plan. Don't be one of them!

Pick your investments with an eye to the bottom line. What is the business plan, and what types of capital do they need to achieve it? Do their financial statements reflect a good use of capital, or do they struggle to make ends meet?

Consider using the Rule of 72. Einstein, who believed that one of the wonders of the world was compounding interest, came up with the rule. He explained that if you divide 1 into 72, then you get 72. So, if an investment pays 1% of interest, then it will take you 72 years to double your money. Now if that same investment paid you 72% interest, then it would only take you one year to double your money.

Recognize that there are wealth killers. These are taxes and inflation. Working with professionals, you can find ways to legitimately reduce your tax bill. Inflation, however, is not something that you can easily control. Therefore, in the Rule of 72, it is important to use a 3% percentage for inflation. Essentially, now you divide 3 into 72 and you come up with 24. That means in 24 years, the price of everything will have doubled. Therefore, when you are determining whether an investment is a good idea, you have to think about whether your return will be greater than the inflation during the same period. If not, then it is not going to help increase your wealth but may actually decrease it.

It is a question of finding the right type of investments that can work for you, based on your investment knowledge and risk tolerance.

Additionally, certain investments can create a greater tax liability based on the percentage of income earned. Therefore, you need to work with a tax professional to determine the best ways to legally minimize your tax bill through deductions. You may also choose to sell an investment to keep your income percentage lower and thus reduce your tax liabilities.

Many individuals argue about the amount of taxes they pay, or see them as excessive. I am not saying that those things might not be true, but at this point, governments depend on the tax revenue paid by their citizens. Here is a point that I thought was interesting from the New Testament of the Bible. Jesus was approached by the Pharisees and asked whether he should pay a temple tax. Now the Jews had no love for Roman taxes, and Jesus knew that their motive was to try to trip him up.

Instead, Jesus had one of his disciples pull out a coin and he asked whose face was on the coin. When the Pharisees responded that it was Caesar, Jesus responded, "Render therefore unto Caesar the things which are Caesar's, and unto God the things that are God's." The point? That taxes and the expenses associated with them are what we render to the government for the services it provides. At the same time, we can render receipts or other documentation to reduce what we owe, just as I am doing to have a $20,000 tax bill adjusted.

Therefore, whether you like it or not, these taxes are going to reduce your gross monthly income for years to come. However, there are ways to reclaim some of that money through your tax-deductible expenses. Working with a tax professional, you can find the best way to do so, recognizing that there are legal ways to effectively reduce your tax bill.

Another point to remember is that not all income is created equally. What do I mean by that? You have interest income, wage income, and rental income, for example. Each of those can result in a different tax rate, with different deductions that are applicable, as well as different rules for what must be reported. Recognize that you need to understand where your money is coming from to achieve the wealth goals that you want in your life.

Our next section is going to focus on Out of Wealth Expenses (OWE), which is where the income meets the expenses.

OUT OF WEALTH EXPENSES (OWE)

Your income is your wealth, and it provides you a means to pay for the things you need and want. These expenses typically reduce your wealth over the course of the month. When you think of this aspect of the blueprint, think of it as breathing out, expelling your financial capital in a variety of ways.

Take a moment and write down all of your monthly expenses. The list is going to include your mortgage or rent, utilities, car payment, insurance, internet, cell phone, and whatever else drains your income throughout the month. There are also those incidentals that you don't think about, because they have become automatic. Your stop at the coffee shop in the morning for that amazing latte? Out of wealth expense. Your regular lunch out with your workmates? Out of wealth expense. These little expenses can add up significantly over the course of a month. You might want to consider making note of every dollar you spend over the course of the week. You may be surprised at how much money simply disappears without you being consciously aware of it.

Remember **ATEMS**:

A – Accommodations

T – Transportation

E – Entertainment

M – Meals

S – Spending

Each of these has an impact on your budget. For instance, accommodations often take the largest chunk of your budget, with transportation next, then entertainment, communications, data, meals, and other spending. This type of spending could even include buying chocolate from a child for a fundraiser at school. Other expenses can include everything from lottery tickets to coffee and medical bills.

Now, there are other expenses that many of us deal with. Student loans, credit card debt, and perhaps even medical expenses. All of it adds up and can significantly reduce your income. There are ways to reduce those expenses, including refinancing loans for a lower interest rate or reducing your credit card spending. You also need to find ways to pay down debt faster, because this will save you money in the long run. What do I mean by that?

Most debts involve paying some form of interest on the debt. It is how the lenders make money from the individuals that they lend to. Now some interest rates are smaller than others, and obviously, the better your credit score the lower the interest rate is likely to be. Why? Because the higher credit scores are seen as lower risk to the lender, hence they receive the benefits in terms of lower interest payments.

However, when your credit score is lower, your interest is typically higher, and it costs you more to borrow money. The best way to save money on interest is to pay more than the minimum and apply as much as possible to the principal of the loan. Doing so will reduce the amount of interest paid over time. I have seen several examples of individuals who end up paying thousands of dollars in interest on their credit cards, simply because they refuse to make more than the minimum payments. Do not fall into this trap.

The best way to save money on interest is to negotiate a better rate, and always pay more than the minimum. When you are offered great credit offers, be sure to read the fine print. You may find that if you cannot pay the balance in full by the end of the term, you may be facing higher interest fees.

Once you pay down debt, it is important to keep it down. There are two types of debt: the type that is for non-assets and the debt for assets. The reason this difference is key is because, when you create debt to buy assets, you are building your net worth. When you grow non-asset debt, you are actually reducing your net worth and lowering your wealth.

If you have written all those expenses down, including food, gas, and what you spend on clothes, then you know what your out of wealth expenses are. Is that out of wealth number lower or higher than your net income? If it is higher, then you are in good shape and can start looking for ways to increase that income even further through investing.

However, if your net income is below your out of wealth expenses, then you are going to have to make some adjustments before you can start actively building wealth. The first step was already done when you listed all your expenses. Look over that list and don't make anything safe. Everything has the potential to be cut. For instance, those coffee shop visits? Perhaps they need to be on the chopping block to give you back more of your net income.

Anything that is an expense should be on this list, but keep in mind that choosing your expenses can mean you save money, or you might find that you are spending more than you need to in terms of taxes.

Look at your credit card debt. Are you getting your credit cards paid down, only to spend on them again, perhaps even drawing them over the limit regularly? All of these areas are places that you can start to reduce your out of wealth expenses. The point of this exercise is not to deprive you of the things that make life enjoyable, but to look for ways to make your net income and your out of wealth expenses balance. Eventually, the goal is to make sure that your out of wealth expenses are significantly lower than your net income.

One of the ways to do so is by tracking your expenses. If an expense is tax deductible, keep the receipt and then use that deduction when you file your taxes. To do this effectively, keep all your receipts and then separate them with your accountant into two piles, tax deductible and non-deductible. You might be surprised at how many deductions you have that you may have never claimed before.

Understand that money for business-related expenses is likely to be tax deductible, but personal items are not. Pay cash for personal items and then borrow for business expenses, thus allowing for the interest paid on business loans to be a tax deduction.

Think D=Deductible and ND=Not Deductible. Clearly, you can see the benefits of being a part-time business owner, even while you are an employee. Still, to be sure that you are getting all the tax benefits from your deductions and to determine which ones you qualify for, please consult with a tax professional.

Why do you think the rich become rich and stay that way? Because they tailor their lifestyle to a portion of their net income and then stick to it. They look for means to bring down their tax bill and do the recordkeeping necessary to achieve that. Additionally, they look for ways to increase that income, which leads me to Assets (A).

ASSETS (A)

To put it bluntly, assets are what you could sell to pay your debts. It could be your home, your car, or other valuables, such as jewelry. All of these items are assets. Your ability to purchase new assets can be based on your net income, but purchasing assets allows you to grow your net worth.

Investments can be a way to create assets. For instance, you might have $100,000 to invest. Now you could buy a rental property free and clear for that amount, or you could take that same amount and use it for down payments on four other properties. The result is that you have significantly increased your net worth by the value of those assets, but you have also increased your monthly net income due to the rental income.

Assets can be collateral for loans, or a way to get a lower interest rate. Home Equity Lines of Credit (HELOC) are a great way to maximize the asset you have in your home. You can pay the interest only or pay the whole amount off at any time. It allows you flexibility to invest in additional assets over time.

Assets are a critical part of building your wealth. I like to think of them as an acronym for the types of investments out there.

- **A** – Accumulating
- **S** – Several
- **S** - Stocks
- **E** – Estates
- **T** – Trusts
- **S** – Securities

Note that the point of accumulating these things is to create wealth, by the income they produce and the value they have against the debt that you might carry to purchase them. Choosing your investments wisely can help you to increase your assets and positively impact your net worth. Every investment has a level of risk, but the point is to balance your level of risk with the return from that investment.

In real estate, for example, you are focusing on being cash flowing on a property. That means the property covers its own expenses and still provides a positive income to you. I want you to remember that investments will have losses from time to time, but the point is that you don't want to have to continue to put income into an investment, because if it is not increasing in value, you are losing money.

I want you to get off your ass and do something to achieve something.

Are you willing to step outside of your comfort zone and try different investments? It might include spending assets to build your own business. The value of the business can grow, thus giving you an asset for your hard work.

I pointed this out because your ability to grow your income and purchase assets will be limited by your net income. When you work a traditional wage job, it caps your net income by the hours you work and the size of your paycheck. I am here to tell you that business ownership can mean taking your net income and growing it with no cap.

Now you might not be comfortable running a business, or you might be unsure of how certain things work when it comes to running a business. However, that is why you need to be willing to work with professionals. They can supply the knowledge and experience you lack. Plus, you don't want to be doing every job involved in running a business. You do not have enough time or energy to achieve all of that. The term is delegating, and it is key to any successful business.

Remember, you are doing something to achieve the wealth you want. Start looking at business opportunities with a critical eye. What is the investment needed, and the potential rate of return? How long before the business would be cash flowing? You might find, for example, that a franchise offers you the ability to purchase a business with all the systems in place, which may reduce your initial investment. However, franchises can also limit your ability to make changes as you see fit.

Therefore, it is important to weigh your options before choosing a business to invest in or purchase outright. Plus, when you purchase a business, you take on liabilities as well. However, liabilities are littered throughout the different types of assets available.

Let's move on to Liabilities (L) and how they can impact your wealth.

LIABILITIES (L)

Part of the point of liabilities is understanding that they are the items that reduce your net worth and negatively impact your wealth. Granted, they might be necessary expenses, but the point is that they are reducing the amount of net income you have to build your wealth.

You can think of them as sunk costs, ones that you are not likely to recoup as part of your investments and wealth building strategy. It could be insurance, setting up a trust or will, and consulting with professionals to determine the best tax strategy for your circumstances. The point is that these expenses are not going to be recovered, but the amount of these expenses also needs to be monitored. You might find yourself spending more than you should on sunk costs, and that can negatively impact your wealth.

However, the real liability is when you lie about your abilities, and you limit what you are capable of. So, you take advice from broke friends and family members, instead of consulting with those individuals who are professionals and experienced in generating wealth. Here is where I want to encourage you to look for mentors or coaches, and follow them.

They have experience and knowledge that you might not, but they also can help you to capitalize on the knowledge and experience that you already have. These mentors have walked the path that you are starting down, and can be critical to helping you achieve your goals and objectives. These are the individuals that can give you encouragement, and can also hold you accountable for achieving what is possible in your life.

CREATING TARGETS TO ACHIEVE YOUR VISION

When it comes to creating more income, you want to have several different targets. I think of them as the minimum, the medium, and the maximum. The minimum is essentially what you are making as a net income right now, factoring in wage increases or perhaps additional investment income. Now you might set your minimum as slightly higher, so you have a goal to shoot for in terms of increasing your net income from month to month.

The medium is a larger goal, outside of your comfort zone, that makes you have to hustle a bit to achieve it. You might take on an extra project for additional income beyond your job, or you might find yourself investing more. The point of medium is to make you stretch yourself further than you have before. To achieve your goals in terms of growing your wealth, you need to be willing to step outside of your comfort zone. Medium goals are meant to be a driver for that. At the same time, when you achieve a medium goal, you feel the rush that comes from accomplishing something and it pumps you up. Suddenly, you can see that more is possible. That is where the maximum comes in.

Now I have heard this goal referred to as outrageous, but the point is that this goal means you are really going to have to stretch yourself and take a gigantic leap outside of your comfort zone. It might even mean completely changing your lifestyle to break the barriers keeping you from reaching that maximum goal. From month to month, you are going to be able to reach plenty of minimum goals and even a few of the mediums, but you might think that the maximum goals are just too far out of reach.

I am here to tell you that is not the case. In fact, every time you reach a medium goal, you put that maximum goal closer and make it easier to reach. Even if you don't achieve it right away, you don't feel like a failure, because you achieved one of your other goals. The point is to put achievement on a sliding scale, making it easier to keep yourself pumped up to achieve the financial goals and dreams that you have always envisioned.

Part of this process involves changing how you think about building wealth. You want to use your income to generate future income. Your wealth is going to be tied to the investment choices you make and how you use those investments to essentially fund the purchase of future investments. If your investments have investments of their own and you are living off of that income, you are generating a consistent income stream that will positively impact your net wealth for years to come.

As an investor, you also have the opportunity to have your money start making money for you by using a professional. It is important to remember that there are individuals out there who spend their days working hard at finding the right investments to fit a variety of circumstances or investing goals. They are going to listen to your vision and help you make smart investment choices to achieve it.

Interview people and find the ones who are successful. For instance, if you decide to use a financial planner, ask how much they made last year. If it was less than you, then that is not the person you want working with you, because he is broke! You want to work with successful people to achieve your own success.

One of the key points I want you to understand from this chapter is that, as an employee, everyone is benefiting financially but you! Self-employed individuals pay the same tax rate as employed individuals, but they get to take deductions not available to employees, plus they have a more flexible schedule. Business owners get even more deductions and tax incentives. Optimize your income by owning a business. If you are thinking that owning a business is time-consuming and you don't have the time, consider hiring a general manager to run the business for you. For more information about the benefits of business ownership to your financial success, visit my website, www.transformationalblueprints.com.

Then you receive the benefits of owning the business, while being able to collect the income and still pursue what you enjoy in life.

Your circumstances can also change throughout your life, meaning that your financial vision is altered as well. Working with professionals can help you to keep your investments in line with your vision, even as it changes throughout your lifetime.

CREATING YOUR FINANCIAL BLUEPRINT

Finally, I want to discuss how this all can impact the life that you live. Many of us have dreams and goals, but the financial realities are limiting us from achieving them. I want you to be able to live the life you have always dreamed of, and fulfill your purpose. To do so, you need financial resources. When you choose to work with a financial professional, you get access to someone who can help you to achieve the financial resources necessary to achieve your dreams.

You have the ability to create an amazing life, but you have to believe that you are worth it. Once you make that conscious decision, then the next step is to define what amazing is to you. Everyone's idea of an amazing life is different, depending on their own personal experiences, beliefs, and values.

I want you to take a minute and define an amazing life for yourself. I can give you one example of how I value myself, and what I believe is a critical part of my amazing life. I always travel first class. Now, it is more expensive than a seat in economy or business class, but I value myself and see it as a priority not to spend hours cramped as I fly. Granted, this might not be one of your priorities, but that is what makes this part so interesting. All of us are unique, and so each of our lives can be amazing based on those unique aspects.

Get excited about the possibilities. Define your amazing life and then act to create it. If you wait for someone else to give it to you, you will be waiting a long time. My mother is still incredibly active, living life to the fullest. It is an example that inspires me to get the most out of every day of my life.

I also want to stress the importance of finding support to create real change in your financial life. After all, it isn't going to be easy to change how you view money, how you interact with it, and how you invest it. In fact, you might be so focused on just paying this month's bills that you can't even imagine life more than 30 days from now. That is the mentality that you need to break. It takes conscious effort to create that mental change, to shift your mindset.

After all, it took years to create the habits and mindset that are now your automatic default. When you change the default, it takes time to make it permanent. To be successful at it, you must get started. Financial shifts require effort as well, but they are so worth it. Do not be quick to assume that you can't do it! Instead, focus on the blueprint and your action steps in each area. Perhaps you just focus on one area at first, then shift to another. Over time, you will see the change, and its impact on your life.

Throughout this chapter, I have shared key strategies and important information that can help you through the process of creating wealth and growing your net worth. It comes down to a simple formula, one that requires you to think in terms of algebraic equations. (And you said that you would never use that again!)

Income – Out of Wealth Expenses = Your Net Wealth

Assets – Liabilities = Your Net Worth

These two points are essentially your financial blueprint. No matter what you do financially, it fits into one of these four categories. The point is to make smart choices that positively impact these areas and thus increase your financial wellbeing. Go to BernardI.O.A.L..com to find more information on how this financial blueprint can help you to achieve success.

What are some ways that you can make real change in these areas? Let's look at all of them one at a time.

- **Income** – Look for ways to increase your income through investments or business ownership. These options allow you to use your money to make more money, instead of just putting more hours in at a job. Remember, you can only work so many hours a week, which naturally limits how much income potential is available at a traditional job.

- **Out of Wealth Expense** – Choose your priorities and then work to manage your out of wealth expenses. Always remember to live within your net income, not your gross income!

- **Assets** – Building a portfolio of assets is key to growing your net worth. Choose your assets, not only for their current value, but for how those assets can grow over time. Work with a professional financial manager to help you invest effectively to increase your net worth and build income streams that allow you to live the life you want.

- **Liabilities** – Not all liabilities are the same. Some are the result of doing business, including insurance and legal or tax guidance. Limit liabilities that drain your resources unnecessarily.

Each of these areas is part of making your finances what you need them to be in order to achieve an amazing life. I have focused on your mindset, on your choices, and on ways you can create real change. However, they all require you to get up and move. You need to act, to embrace your abilities, and focus on what you are capable of.

Too many of us sell ourselves short and end our lives wondering what we missed out on, because we did not embrace our abilities and talents. Don't make that mistake!

Granted, you might not be interested in an investment because it doesn't mix with your values or it is not going to get you where you want to go in the timeframe you have already defined. The point is to explore the options and find the ones that work for you.

I met a wealthy friend who told me about a great book, Rich Dad Poor Dad by Robert Kiyosaki. That book opened my eyes to so many concepts that before had appeared complicated. It was as I read his book and took inspiration from it that I had a better understanding of income and how to generate it, as well as the tax implications of that. Today, I help people determine the best investments based on their goals, helping them to understand how each income presents different tax rates and more.

Now is the time to act. Don't put it off until tomorrow or some future date that will never come. Instead, open your mind to the possibilities.

Years ago, a friend interviewed for a position as an office boy. It was going well, until she asked for his email address and he explained that he didn't have one. She politely said they couldn't use him, and that was the end of the interview. Instead of allowing a fear of rejection and the accompanying dejection take hold, he decided to get active.

He had $10, so he went to a wholesale fruit distributor and bought a bag full of produce. He then sold it door to door. That day, he doubled his money and a new venture was born. It took time, but he went from walking to riding a bicycle to owning a truck and then a fleet of trucks. His hard work created a viable business. Now, he could have let that interview bring him down but, instead, he used it as inspiration to move forward. I want to provide that same inspiration to you. I want to help you act to create your vision. Don't let the rejection get you and keep you from fulfilling your dreams and goals!

Let's get started working together as a TEAM (Together Everyone Achieves More). Please contact me at my website, www.transformationalblueprints. com, to create real change in your financial life, and discovering the resources to fund the amazing life that you deserve! In this chapter, I have shared how to map out your financial plan, creating a You Are Here point in your life. Now I need you to transform this moment, getting rid of what no longer serves you by transforming your thoughts and feelings, essentially exhaling your negative thoughts and emotions.

Part of that process involves taking action. What do you want to be known for at the end of your life? Name three things. Now is the time to create and build, so use those three things as a platform to get started. Let them help you to craft your mission statement and the theme song of your life. You are in control of your mind's eye, your dreams, and your creativity. These are the tools that will allow you to reach your destination and leave a legacy behind for generations.

Practice conscious bio-breathing. Take a moment to think about what you love, and then hold that breath and truly experience your thoughts. Recognize that in that very moment, there are thousands of cells are being born in your body! All those cells with be filled with the energy and information captured in your DNA. Now exhale on the negativity in your life, including jealousy, visualizing the cells dying and leaving your body within the time it takes to exhale. It is all mind over matter. If you don't mind, then it don't matter!

Life is a journey of experiences, but you are the one who takes those experiences and crafts them into a truly amazing life, one that will be a legacy for others to follow for generations!

Please go to www.transformationalblueprints.com to download the I.O.A.L. chart and to get more information and details about Bernard H. Dalziel.

The Scary Truth About Lost Opportunity Cost

MITZY DADOUN, MASTER ASA, CPCA

If what you thought was true turned out not to be true, when would you want to know? My friend and business associate, Don Blanton from MoneyTrax, starts most of his seminars with this question. It really stops and makes you think.

We all go through life making decisions based on our value system of what's right and what's wrong. We assess situations and information based on the knowledge we've gained from the past—knowledge from family, school, friends, business associates, religion and our own experiences. We make our decisions based on this information.

Often the people we rely on for information are giving us the best information they can, but they may not have the background or the resources to really help us assess this particular situation. Our parents, for example, grew up in an era where people frequently worked for the same company their entire life, and they retired from that company with a pension. Our parents often lived in one house their entire adult life with one mortgage that they quickly worked to pay off. We live in very different times. People are much more mobile, and tend not to work for the same company for their entire career. Even if someone works for a company for a long time, can they actually retire and know that that company pension is secure? How can that pension be secure when so many "companies that will be around forever" are gone (Eaton's, Sears, Simpson's and Kodak to name a few)? Given the huge differences between our generation and the last, isn't it doubtful that our parents have the information we need to solve any number of challenges?

Technology is also rapidly changing our world. The jobs that were once stable are becoming obsolete and new jobs are being invented daily. What worked for our parents is often the exact opposite of what may work for us. We're in an ever-changing world—a world that's very different when compared to the world our parents grew up in, and it's a world much different than our kids will grow up in. What will work for us may not work for our children.

The reality is that often we don't have all of the necessary information when we're making our decisions. We're making them based on the facts we have at the time, not on the entire picture. The best example of this is the following simple ride on the subway.

It's a beautiful peaceful day. There are five or six other people sitting in the subway car. A gentleman gets onto the car with his five children and they are simply wild. He seems to be sitting there in a daze, not caring about the way his children are behaving. As the train is going from stop to stop, you can feel the tension of all the other people getting higher and higher. Finally, it gets to the point where I say something to the gentleman. "Excuse me sir, I hate to bother you but your kids seem to be going wild. Could you please speak to them and see if you can quiet them down?"

He kind of stops and shakes his head and comes out of his daze. Then he says, "Oh, I'm so sorry, their mother just died. We just left the hospital. I guess they just don't know what to do."

In that split second, I went from wanting to strangle the man to wanting to wrap my arms around him and comfort him in any way I could. In an instant I went from wanting to have those children be disciplined to feeling so sorry them.

(From Steven Covey's 7 Habits for Highly Effective People. It stays with me on a daily basis.)

Think about the following:

How did you feel when you heard about the rowdy kids? How did you feel about the father ignoring his wild children who were disturbing everyone? What thoughts came into your mind? And how did you feel after you found out why the man and his children were acting like this?

In a split second you had a paradigm shift, a complete and total change of how you felt and what you thought. The facts were always the same! You thought you had all the facts but you didn't. Please make the effort to keep this story in mind as you go through your day and as you encounter people. Maybe that rude cashier just received some horrible news. Be kind, you never know what's going on in someone else's world. A smile and a kind word can make all the difference in the world to someone going through a difficult time.

I'm very lucky I grew up in a safe and great city: Kingston, Ontario. Growing up, my grandmother and aunt always told me they believed in me, that I could do anything I set my mind to. I had an amazing teacher in grade seven, Sharon Bullock (Deline), who saw more in me than I saw in myself at the time. She really went the extra mile and helped me through a hard time in my life. I hope each of you is blessed enough to have at least one of those teachers in your life, a teacher who looks below the surface and really cares about and invests in their students.

I went away to a university that helped me start the process of expanding my mind, but I think my eyes really opened up to possibilities when I travelled and saw how different various parts of the world were. I visited historic sites and learned how advanced past civilizations were. How things like flushing toilets existed (albeit in a slightly different fashion), thousands of years ago. (I hated history in school but love it as an adult—I think the difference is my history teacher just stated the facts, but when you go somewhere, you bring it to life.)

I was lucky when I started my working career. I started working for a gentleman named Scott Cameron at Mutual Trust. He encouraged me to go to courses and expand my mind, to listen to and read Zig Ziglar, Jim Rohn, Napoleon Hill, Brian Tracy, Jay Abraham, Mark Victor Hansen, Robert Kyosoki, Raymond Aaron, Tony Robbins, John Maxwell and so many others. Over the years I listened to many great speakers who got me thinking and expanding my mind. They say most people read just one or two books after they finish school and hardly ever go to seminars. I've read thousands of books, listened to thousands of seminars and podcasts and attended hundreds of seminars in person. I'm something of an information junkie, as my husband says.

There's so much more out there than most of us realize. I encourage you to go to or listen to a seminar on a topic you haven't studied before. Expand your mind with new knowledge in new areas. If you haven't heard about or listened to Ted Talks I encourage you to do so. You can listen to talks on almost any topic and you can use the app to find any topic for any amount of time. You can listen to a 5-minute talk on astrophysics while you brush your teeth or a 20-minute talk on solutions to world hunger. Have fun, expand your mind.

ANOTHER PARADIGM SHIFT

The rich do things differently than the average person does. If we look at the population of the United States, over 70 percent of people earn under $75,000 a year. What this means is the wealth-building strategies you see on TV and hear on the radio are put out to the masses for those people who are earning under $75,000 a year.

The wealth-building strategies that people who are earning over $75,000 a year use are different from most other strategies. Robert Kiyosaki is famous for many books, the first being *Rich Dad, Poor Dad*. He goes through the different strategies that the rich use versus the masses. Napoleon Hill, in his book *Think and Grow Rich*, talks about the strategies for building long-term generational wealth. He talks about both mindset and the actions we take. Don Blanton is another brilliant mind, and his groundbreaking book *The Personal Economic Model* is an absolute must read for anyone. Don's book will help you see the strategies that are employed by the very wealthy, the strategies that everyone can use but historically only the wealthy have had access to and used. These are the models I use with my clients at Wealth Creation Concepts, employing uncommon strategies that help build long-term generational wealth, and create the financial security so many desire.

LOST OPPORTUNITY COST (LOC)

One of the biggest concepts that most people are unaware of is Lost Opportunity Cost, or LOC.

LOC can be explained by saying if you have a dollar, you have the ability to invest that dollar, and it has the ability to grow over time, but if you lose that dollar unknowingly and unnecessarily to taxes, interest on credit cards, etc., then not only do you lose that actual dollar but you lose the opportunity cost of what it could have grown into if you still had it. We all know we have to pay taxes, that's an opportunity cost we can't avoid, but we can work to minimize those taxes. We can work to ensure that we build our wealth as much as possible keeping that in mind.

You have two choices with every dollar you earn; you can spend it or you can save and invest it. If you earn 5 percent when you invest a dollar, your dollar will grow over time and become part of the engine that builds your wealth. If you spend the dollar, it will become part of someone else's engine.

A dollar is not just a dollar. It's also the interest you could have earned on that dollar as it grew over time. The LOC is what that dollar could have grown to.

Every dollar we earn has to go through a huge wealth sucking filter. First, the government filters off their tax. Second, we can spend and enjoy the remaining money, invest and save it for the future or do a combination thereof.

QUALIFIED SAVINGS PLANS

A qualified savings plan is known as an RSP or RIF in Canada and a 401k in the United States. Most people look at such plans and think, these are great! They think they can put money into the plan and the government won't charge them any taxes. What people forget is that they are just deferring the taxes, not eliminating them. They're sending that money to be assessed down the road.

When you put money into an RRSP, RIF or 401k, you're investing the money and any losses or gains that occur affect its value, but the taxes will be assessed only in the future.

If down the road you are in a lower tax bracket than when you put the money into the investment, you'll pay less in tax than if you had paid the tax right away. If, however, you're in a higher tax bracket, you'll pay more in tax. When you go to use the money in your retirement, or when you withdraw it for any reason, you'll be taxed based on the tax bracket you're

[1]http://www.cru.org/train-and-grow/devotional-life/personal-guide-to-fasting.2.html

in at the time you withdraw it. The tax man will come and he'll want the government's share of your money.

When you die and there's money in your qualified plan, you can usually roll it over to your spouse, tax deferred, but when it moves to the next generation it comes out as income and will often result in it being taxed at the highest rate possible.

Of course there are times when you can use the deferral to your benefit. Let's say you just got married and you're planning on having kids in five years and your spouse makes significantly more money than you do. The higher earner can put his or her money into a spousal RRSP. Then, the lower earner can withdraw the money based on their reduced tax rate at the proper time. Careful planning is required here because there are attribution rules. The spouse can't contribute to the spousal RRSP in the year you withdraw the money or the two preceding years. You can also put money into your own RRSP and withdraw the money during those years you know you will have little or no other income.

When you make contributions to a qualified plan you have to think about your current tax bracket and your likely future tax bracket. If you're in a higher tax bracket when you withdraw the money, you could actually end up paying a higher tax rate on that money than you would have if you had just paid the tax up front. Most people don't look at and think about the fact that the tax calculation is going to happen down the road. In effect you have set up a joint bank account with the government, you take all the risk and they tell you down the road how much of your money they want and how fast.

Think about it, right now the Canadian and the American governments have large, looming tax bills, are greatly in debt, have aging infrastructure, an aging population and they've convinced people to invest in tax deferred (which most people think are tax free) plans. Where will it be easiest to get money in the future? Where will it be easiest to increase taxes? The governments will simply increase the tax rates at the time when you go to withdraw that money.

WHAT THE RICH PEOPLE DO

People earning over $75,000 a year and certainly people in the top 5 percent of earnings and net worth do not rely solely on their RRSP's, RIFS and 401Ks, but rather on several strategies that, when combined, reduce tax, reduce LOC, preserve wealth and transfer their wealth to their children and to their favourite charities.

How many people think that with government debt levels where they are, government spending increasing, health care costs on the rise and the many natural disasters that have occurred and will occur, the governments will be lowering tax rates substantially over time for the "average" Canadian or American?

Tax free savings accounts in Canada and Roth 401k plans in the United States allow people to invest money with their after-tax dollars and have the growth on that money be tax free. I think it's an excellent program because you're paying the tax now, you know what it's going to be and it gives you the control on your investments.

LIQUIDITY USE AND CONTROL

When your money is in a tax-free savings account you can access it during an emergency. There are several other phenomenal financial tools where you can get multiple benefits from each dollar you invest. Knowing which tools to use when and how to combine them is key.

I think one of the things that people forget, especially in regard to qualified plans, is that you have a partner, the government. You have a partner that lets you take all of the losses, shares in all of the gains, and tells you how much of your money they want at a future date.

Let's say I offer to loan you $20,000. You are probably going to want to know what rate of interest I'm going to charge and how fast I want my principal back. What if I told you that "things are good right now, just take the money"? I'll let you know down the road what the interest rate is and how fast I want my money back. Would you take the $20,000 if you were obligated to pay back an unknown amount in the future? I might charge you a 20 percent interest rate or a 40 percent interest rate (tax bracket). That's exactly what happens with a qualified plan. The government loans you the tax money and reserves the right to change tax rates and withdrawal rates whenever and however they want.

YOU FINANCE EVERYTHING YOU BUY

You either pay interest on it or you give up the ability to earn interest on that money. If you pay cash for something, you lose the opportunity cost of what that money could have earned. If you finance it with a mortgage or a loan, you pay interest on the money, but you still have your money in your account earning interest.

One of the main reasons people like to pay cash for things is because they don't want to pay interest because in their minds they see it as losing money. The truth is you could actually be losing money if you pay cash because you lose the opportunity cost on that money and, depending on what the interest rate is and on what you finance, you could do better with your investments. I'll give you an example right now using a car.

Say you have the ability to finance a car. There are a lot of car companies that are currently offering 0 percent or 1.99 percent financing on cars. Now, say you have invested your money in a mutual fund, real estate or in your business and it will earn 6 to 8 percent. If you pay $50,000 for your car, you lose the ability to earn that 6-8 percent on your money. If you finance it you pay 0 percent interest, you spread out the payments over time and have the ability for your money to keep earning interest and growing. You also retain use and control of your money so if some kind of emergency occurs you can access the money. In this particular scenario it could very well make sense to finance the car using other people's money. If you're self-employed and can write off the loan, it makes even more sense. You're better off to take the loan from the car company! You get to keep, use and control your $50,000. You have flexibility if there's an emergency because you still have the cash available. You aren't giving up anything except for that monthly payment that you have to make. You'll also have the $50,000 in your bank account that you could use to pay off the loan if you wanted to.

YOUR MORTGAGE

One of the biggest assets most people have during their life is their home and one of the biggest expenses most people have is their mortgage. I want you to really stop and think about this. I'm going to share some very uncommon information, but it's probably one of the biggest areas where the rich do things very differently than most of people do.

THINK ABOUT THESE QUESTIONS

If you put down a large down payment on your home, will you save more than if you put a small down payment? If you have a 15-year amortization on your mortgage versus a 30-year amortization on your mortgage, will you save money? What about if you make lots of extra payments on your mortgage? If you answered yes to any of those questions you are about to have a paradigm shift.

I WANT YOU TO REALLY PAY ATTENTION TO THIS NEXT SECTION.

Let's say you buy a house (A) for $500,000 and you pay 100 percent cash for it, and I buy a house (B) for $500,00 and I finance it 100 percent. The houses are side-by-side and exactly the same. It's now five years down the road and houses in your area have gone up by 10 percent. The value of house A went up by 10 percent and the value of house B went up by 10 percent. Did it make a difference how much the down payment was or how much financing was needed to buy the house? No. The two houses went up by exactly the same amount. They are both now worth $550,000. They went up exactly the same whether the house was owned 100 percent outright or if it was 100 percent financed.

I'm not saying you can finance your house 100 percent and even if you could I'm not saying you should, but what I'm saying is this is one major area where the wealthy do something very different. The rich will finance the property 65 to 75 percent so that they will only be tying up about 25 to 35 percent of their own cash and then using that 65 -75 percent of other people's money and they will deploy and utilize that remaining amount in some other asset where it can also grow and create wealth.

So, if you take that $350,000 and you deploy it somewhere and you earn even 3 percent on your money, you now have your house which grew by 10 percent and you have another asset that grew by 3 percent. Or maybe you invested it in another property that you rent out and it will grow by 10 percent as well. Now you have two assets building your wealth. What about all the interest you have to pay on the mortgage? It's true you'll have to pay the interest on that mortgage but don't forget the lost opportunity cost comes into the equation as well. If you paid cash for the house you lose the opportunity cost of the cash you used to pay for the house. The house will go up in value the same amount whether it is paid for 100 percent or financed 100 percent. The increase in value on the real estate is not dependant on the down payment.

REAL ESTATE

Real estate has historically been one of the biggest areas where people have built great wealth. There are several great strategies to help you accumulate wealth with real estate. Real estate, when combined with the right type of permanent insurance, creates the ultimate combination for wealth creation and preservation.

INSURANCE

Insurance is another area where people often lose money unknowingly and unnecessarily. Some types of insurance are pure cost but necessary: car insurance, house insurance, term insurance, liability insurance, etc. Some types of insurance offer additional benefits and can be coordinated with other assets to shelter income, defer tax and even eliminate taxes. Knowing what type to use and when can make a significant difference in your wealth and financial security.

Building wealth requires:

1. spending less than you make

2. building an emergency fund

3. protecting your assets

4. paying down debt

5. utilizing strategies that help your dollars do more than one job at a time so that your investments grow as much as possible

6. minimizing taxes while accumulating wealth, when accessing the wealth in your retirement and upon your death

When you are looking at accumulating and preserving wealth you can think of it like a golf game. Would you rather have the skills of the best golfers or the clubs of the best golfers? Ideally you would have both!! The strategies I use with my clients are the skills, the various products are the clubs. Do you always use the driver or the putter? No. They do different things but are both extremely important. The driver represents the rate of return on your investments. It has the potential to go the furthest but is hard to control. The putter on the other hand does not hit the ball far but is easy to control and very often games are won or lost based on the puts made or lost. You can be winning the game for 18 holes and lose it all because of a bad put!! Properly structured permanent life insurance is the putter.

If you would like to learn more about these strategies, go to **www.WealthCreationConcepts.com** where you can request a phone or in person meeting. You can also call or text Mitzy at 416-993-2532.

Be the best you can be.

Ask yourself, "If what I think is true turns out not to be true, when would I want to know?"

Immigrating to Success

Self-Leadership Strategies to Manifest Your Life Long Dreams

JACEK SIWEK

Immigration requires more than interest, it requires commitment. If you want to immigrate to success, commitment is a must.

Some decisions in life make little difference, others will turn your life around entirely. For example, a decision to immigrate is definitely a life-changing decision. I left Poland and immigrated to Canada in 1996. My whole life changed in just one day. I had to learn a new language and culture, gain new friends, learn how to live in a big city, and the list goes on and on. However, there was one more decision I made that had a significant impact on my life. It was the decision to be successful. It wasn't an easy journey, but now that I look back in time, I see how immigrating to another country and changing my life from poverty to success resemble each other remarkably. Allow me to explain.

Immigration is a point of no return. It's not a short visit to see how things will work out. If it gets hard you can't go back. An immigrant makes it happen no matter how hard it gets or how long it takes. It's only when you decide with the same amount of certainty to immigrate to success do you have a chance to transform your life.

Why do people immigrate? Most do it to stop or avoid pain. There's a moment in life when you realize that the past was horrible, the present is even more painful, and the future looks worse. At that moment you decide to change. At that moment there's a psychological shift when you say "No more! Not another day of this! This must change and I must change it!"

If I can teach you any lesson about pain, it would be this: pain is the greatest teacher and motivator of all. If you want to succeed in life, you must first get dissatisfied with your current situation. You must experience massive, immediate, enormous, unbearable amounts of pain in order to be able to come to the moment when you realize "This must change!"

If you aren't where you want to be with your finances CHANGE IT. If you aren't where you want to be with your body weight CHANGE IT. If you aren't happy with your job CHANGE IT. If you aren't happy with your relationship CHANGE IT.

Don't get me wrong, I'm all for making the best out of what we have, but far too often I've seen people who suffer being together. I know it's not easy, but it all comes down to that moment of asking "How long do I want to tolerate it?" In life we get what we tolerate, so if you see something isn't working and you keep tolerating it, nothing will change. You must reach the point of no return, the moment when you decide that not another day will pass by with you living like this. This is the perfect moment when you must immigrate to success. There's no better way.

DEFINE YOUR DESTINATION

In order to reach your goal of immigrating to success you must:

1. Clearly define your goals. Define what you want, not what you don't want. You must know exactly when your goal has been achieved.

2. State what you are committed to do in order to achieve your goals.

3. Name the price you are willing to pay to get there (in terms of time, money, and sacrifice).

4. Get rid of old habits that stop you.

5. Identify what it will cost you not to get to where you want to go. What would be the ultimate pain of not getting there?

6. Define who you want to become as a result of achieving this goal.

If you have all those points done your next step is to educate yourself.

FOUR STAGES OF LEARNING

1. *First, you don't know what you don't know.* For example, you have never seen or heard of a car. How could you learn to drive one? You have no clue what it is. Similarly, you might be ignorant to things that could be useful. Someone else must show you what you don't know. Keep your mind open to other possibilities. Remember, you don't have all the

answers.

2. *Second, you know what you didn't know.* At this stage you're discovering the things you weren't aware of. You don't have any skills yet, but you know what you have to learn in order to succeed. For example, you know what a car is and you've seen people driving one, though you have never driven one yourself. In order for you to learn new skills you must not be afraid to ask for help.

3. *Third, you know what you didn't know and you're actually physically doing it.* At this stage you are actively doing what you know, but it takes your full attention. At this stage it will require your entire focus to complete the task. For example, you know what a car is and you know how to drive it, but it takes your full attention and you aren't capable of doing anything else while driving. Now your focus is on your goal, but it's still outside yourself.

4. *Fourth, you are no longer thinking about what you're doing, you're doing it automatically.* At this stage, because of repetition, your subconscious mind is no longer requiring your full attention and focus. You can do the task while focusing on something else. For example, you can drive, but your focus is on something else. You can have a conversation with somebody sitting next to you. You can listen to the radio or you can plan your next day. Your subconscious mind takes over the complex process of operating a vehicle and simplifies it into one task called driving. We call it second nature because we can perform it without our full attention.

HUMILITY

"Be all that you can be." "You're the best." "You can do anything you put your mind to." "Believe in yourself." "You are worth it." We keep hearing these phrases over and over again. You'll find them on the internet, Facebook, YouTube videos, and inside self-improvement books. But what about humility? What is humility? Humility is not thinking less of yourself, but rather it's thinking of yourself less. Read the above sentence a few times until it sinks in. Humility is the greatest friend in your progress and learning.

In the process of immigrating there's something I refer to as you don't know what you already know. It sounds strange, but I'll give you an example. You are quite capable of asking for directions in your own language. However, when you don't know the foreign language it becomes a challenge. Successful people use different language for the same things. They just sometimes use a sophisticated vocabulary. This kind of thing is common in the financial, medical, and legal industries. So when you start spending time with successful people and they use vocabulary you don't understand, do not be discouraged. Chances are you know exactly what they are talking about, but you simply don't know the verbal representations of the discussed topics. Do not be afraid of asking for clarifications.

I know it is humiliating when learning a new language to ask the same question over and over again. You feel stupid asking for something you think you should know by now. But that fear of appearing stupid, that fear of what people will think if you ask this question again, will prevent you from progressing forward. Recognizing this helped me to learn the language and culture faster than many of my peers at the same time. You must know that you need to put your focus on the other person and ask repeatedly for help until you learn those things necessary to succeed. We have to embarrass ourselves many times and be okay with it. We have to give ourselves time to make mistakes—lots and lots of mistakes. If we do, we will progress 100 times faster than those proud people who are too afraid to sound dumb. That's humility working for you.

Being afraid of making mistakes, and looking stupid because of it, is one of the top reasons people don't succeed. If you study successful people you will see a common pattern. They all make a lot of mistakes, experience plenty of failures, feel a lot of embarrassment, and experience a lot of setbacks. If we want to succeed, we must be ready to accept failure as a major part of our path. However, every time you feel like quitting know that there's another person who already quit right behind you. If you keep going forward, there will be fewer people and less competition simply because the reasons they stopped did not stop you. One of the major reasons why people give up or don't try in the first place is because of fear of being humiliated. They don't want people to criticize them, and they don't want people to make fun of them. Nobody does. But the truth is this is your life, and there will always be people who will make fun of you. There will always be people who'll think badly of you, criticize you, and point the finger at you. It's absolutely inevitable. Remember, humility is all about thinking of yourself less, rather than thinking less of yourself.

DIRT REMOVAL

"Bad habits are easier to abandon today than tomorrow."
– Proverb

This step is a must, but you may not appreciate its value until you start putting it in practice. Every house that ever got built started with someone's vision, then a blueprint was made. As much as most want to see the completed version of their beautiful kitchen or bathroom, the first step of construction is removal of dirt. In order to build solid foundations, you must remove all loose soil. You want to build up but first you must go down to the solid place that will not move when storms and winters come. Removal of dirt in your life is no different. We all have it and we must get rid of as much of it as we can in order to build ourselves based on solid value.

Here are some things that might be in your life that aren't allowing you to build the life you want to have:

1. Negative people and their negative comments and criticisms

2. Media. Example: Constant Negative News (CNN)

3. Time wasters: games, social media, TV, excessive entertainment

4. Unfinished projects (like a book you started reading and haven't finished)

5. Disorganized messes (like keys you've never used and don't even know what they're for)

6. Junk food

Removing dirt from your life comes down to one word: STANDARD. You have a standard in life that you'll not go below. A standard is nothing more than a line in the sand that says "I'm not willing to go below this. It's unacceptable, and I refuse to tolerate it." In life we will get what we tolerate, so setting up a minimum standard is a necessity. When I immigrated, all I had with me was one suitcase with summer clothes. When you immigrate, you have to be careful about what you take with you because your allowance for your luggage is limited. At the same time, you'll realize just how few things you really need and that leaving stuff behind might be one of the best things that could happen to free you from having to deal with unnecessary time wasters.

In your new country of success there's simply no space for time wasting activities and negative people.

COMMUNICATE TO INFLUENCE

Every person who ever immigrated to another country knows how difficult it is until they learn the language people use to communicate. If you can't speak the language, your communication will be extremely limited, and as a result your life will always be a struggle. In fact, should someone ask me what the number one skill in life is, I will say without hesitation: "You must master communication skills in order to be successful."

Think about it for a moment. Show me one aspect of your life where proper communication isn't required in order to be successful. If you want to be a successful parent, you must first learn how to communicate with your children. If you want to be a successful spouse, you must learn how to communicate with your partner. If you want to be successful in business, you must learn how to effectively communicate with your customers, employees, business partners, investors, and the list goes on.

However, the most important person you must master communication with is yourself. You have to learn how to communicate with yourself in order to stay motivated, focused, driven, dedicated, and committed. You must know what works for you and what doesn't. You must become a student of yourself first before you learn what motivates others. Language is what connects people, but lack of it separates them. You should put in the effort necessary to learn what you need to know in order to become an effective communicator. Who is an effective communicator? It's a person who can influence others to take action. In order to influence you need to learn how to connect with others first, which means you have to learn how to develop rapport.

MAGIC OF RAPPORT

The key to rapport lies in one word: commonality. I can summarize this skill with one sentence: people like each other when they're like each other. The more you have in common with others the easier it is to develop rapport. Maybe you had a situation when you met someone for the first time and you kept asking questions to find something in common. If you found nothing, then the conversation became awkward and most likely died. Maybe you've known someone for many years and still can't find anything in common, so each time you see each other you feel like you are total strangers. However, I'm also sure you've had a moment in life when you met someone for the first time and instantly felt a connection. After a short period of time you felt like you had known that person forever. Why does that happen? Well, you simply saw yourself in the other person. You liked them because they were like you or they were similar to someone you already liked.

This is all based on commonality. Your subconscious mind will quickly pick up on all the similarities between the person you just met and yourself. If you know nothing of the person you just met, all you have to do is match and mirror them as closely as you can. Immediately match their physiology by copying their body language. If they sit on a chair, you sit on a chair. If they lean forward, you lean forward. If they have crossed legs, you cross yours. Simply match and mirror what they do and their mind will soon start picking up a signal that you are just like them. As soon as they start speaking, match their speaking pattern. If they speak slow, you speak slow. If they speak fast, you speak with the same tempo. You might be afraid they'll notice what you are doing and will accuse you of mimicking them. Truthfully, they won't notice. Especially because they don't know you yet and they don't know your natural behavior. Therefore, the more you copy them the quicker rapport will be developed.

If you use this method daily, sooner or later it will become second nature and you'll be able to develop rapport with people instantaneously without ever worrying about what you'll have to say or how to behave.

PAIN OF LETTING GO

"Sometimes we have to let go of what is good in order to be great."
– Unknown

This moment hits every immigrant on the planet: feeling homesick. It can be missing loved ones, friends, familiar places, or favorite TV shows in your own language. I was not immune to it. I fell in love with a girl right before I immigrated and I missed her a lot. I missed my best friend and our daily walks to school. I missed my town and the street I grew up on. Most of all I missed the feeling of belonging. Everyone has to go through it, but it doesn't make it easier just because others feel the same pain. There were many moments when I felt like just jumping on a plane and going back. Feeling like you want to quit because you feel like you don't belong is normal and eventually will fade away. When you realize that you no longer want to live a life of poverty you'll have to let go of many things, including the ones you love. During the really tough moments when I worked 14 hour days delivering flyers for $2.50 per hour (minimum wage was $8) I kept in mind one thought that kept me going. In order to be great you have to let go of what is good. There's a price to pay for everything and when you immigrate to a new country or to success you will pay a price. There'll be people in your life who were your close friends, and now that you're having success, they won't want to be around you or you won't want to be around them. There'll be people who'll not be happy about your success, not because they don't care about you but because they don't want to be left behind. You'll discover that people who claimed to be your close friends are now starting to see you as an opportunity for their own gain. There'll be moments when you might want to sabotage your success because you'll feel that it's not worth the trouble you're having. But, if you give up struggling for your success, you'll never get there and as a result, you'll never help anyone else to get there either.

Success comes with a price tag and in order to get it there's no other way than to pay the price. However, there's a moment when you'll know how great of a decision you've made by leaving your old way of living and deciding to immigrate. It's the moment when you go back for a visit. After five years of being in Canada, I finally got my papers, so I decided to go back to Poland for a visit. I was sure that all my peers would be far ahead of me because the previous five years I had spent learning how to live again from scratch. Surely a new language, culture, school, group of friends, etc. would have caused me to grow slower than my peers who kept on going. Or so I thought. When I went back, I quickly realized how much I had grown. I saw how many people were still stuck in the same place and had done nothing with their life. If anything, many were worse off than they had been five years previously. This short visit gave me a lot to think about. All of a sudden all the things I missed had smaller value. I still missed my friends and family, but I knew that if I stayed with them my life would never grow forward at the speed it was growing.

One day we went climbing mountains in Poland and came up with an idea to go see Mount Everest the following weekend. Surely enough, the next weekend we were in Nepal looking at the tallest mountain, riding elephants in a jungle, and trekking in one of the most beautiful regions in the world. My peers couldn't even dream about such an adventure. It was then that I realized it all comes down to answering one question: Is it worth it? If the answer is yes, then simply make a decision, find out what it takes, and go for it.

You've most likely heard of people saying that true friends are found in need. Pain or trouble in life will show who your true friends are. There is truth to that, however, success will show you the same. If someone is your true friend, they'll be happy for you when they see you succeeding. Those are the friends you should keep and cherish. Focus on what you've gained and what the true rewards are for your hard work. Your pain of regret will disappear.

ADAPTING TO A NEW CULTURE

"Well, the thing that I learned as a diplomat is that
human relations ultimately make a huge difference."
– Madeleine Albright, the first female U.S. Secretary of State

When you listen to many motivational speakers, some of the most common advice they'll give you is: You have to stand out. You have to be different. You can't be average. Break some rules, etc. There is definitely truth to that, but what they rarely tell you is that in order for you to become valuable you must first learn, practice, and master the fundamentals. What that means is when you immigrate to a new culture you have to learn how they live and do things before you introduce anything new. Simply put, you have to fit in before you stand out.

Gold fish will grow proportionally to the size of the container you put them in. The bigger the container the bigger the fish will grow. We, too, adapt. We want to fit in and be accepted by those we love. Fitting in is by far one of the most powerful internal motivators we have. I'm sure you've heard that we become the average of five of our closest friends. This is a very true statement. Adapting to a new culture first requires choosing the right culture for you. Your friends will create pressure inside you. This internal pressure will become a driving force for you and it could serve you or destroy you.

When a young person goes through army training, they'll often adopt standards and discipline like nowhere else. Very often they'll even keep making their bed and polishing their shoes when they go home where there's no one to ask them to do these things. However, the more time passes the more such useful habits fade away. Why does this happen? Many studies show that people become what their peer group expects them to. That's why choosing the right peer group is so important. This piece of information is so crucial that if you forgot everything else in this chapter and only learned and applied this one principle, your chances of success would be much greater than if you applied everything else in this chapter except this rule.

Nobody successful builds anything meaningful by themselves. You must learn how to build a team of people who have the same vision and surround yourself with those who'll support you on your goals. There's simply no other way. The question is: How do you find people who live in a "successful country?"

Here are some of the things that successful people do versus those who are not:

SUCCESSFUL PEOPLE	UNSUCCESSFUL PEOPLE
Read every day	Watch TV every day
Compliment	Criticize
Embrace change	Fear change
Forgive others	Hold a grudge

SUCCESSFUL PEOPLE	UNSUCCESSFUL PEOPLE
Talk about ideas	Talk about people
Continuously learn	Think they know it all
Accept responsibility for their failures	Blame others for their failures
Have a sense of gratitude	Have a sense of entitlement
Set goals and develop a written life plan	Never set goals
Journal	Claim they journal but never do
Set a budget	Never set a budget
Save money	Spend money rashly
Have mentors and coaches	Have friends to entertain themselves
Hope others will succeed	Hope others will fail
Operate from a transformational perspective	Operate from a transactional perspective
Give other people credit for their victories	Take all the credit for their victories
Share information and data	Hold information and data
Know who they are and who they are not	Not sure who they are
Know their purpose	Don't know their purpose
Exude joy	Exude anger
Wake up early, go to bed early	Wake up late, go to bed late
Listen to educational programs	Listen to news
In control of their life	Out of control of their life
Manage energy	Manage time
Make to be lists	Make to do lists
Certain, focused, outcome oriented	Uncertain, confused, excuses oriented
On track	Lost

SUCCESSFUL PEOPLE	UNSUCCESSFUL PEOPLE
Know realistically where they are in life and where they want to be at a specific point in time	They think they are much further in life than reality and don't know where they want to be
Take care of their body	Pay attention to their body when they get sick
Anticipate change	React to change
They lead by example	They demand from others
They appreciate others, expect from themselves	They expect of others, appreciate nobody
Build themselves by building others	Try to build themselves by putting others down
Train, practice, memorize	Hope to improvise
They say: Thank you for…(doing or being something specific)	They say: Thank you for everything
Know what they want and focus on it	Know what they don't want and focus on it
Speak the truth with consequence	Justify, talk about excuses, lie to get away
Pay full attention	Distracted
They see challenges in life that make them stronger	They see problems in life that make them weaker
Over deliver and exceed people's expectations	Overpromise and under deliver
They keep changing to get better results	They stay the same expecting better results
If something must change I have to change it	If something must change someone else must change it for me
They celebrate their successes	They celebrate holidays only
They have a story of becoming a victor	They have a story of becoming a victim

As you can see these are two different cultures with different beliefs, values, rituals, and habits. The items in the "successful list" are the fundamentals that must be learned and practiced in your network. You might not be able to check off all the things on the list, but the more you do and the more you put them into practice, the quicker you will get where you want to go.

SHORTCUTS THAT SLOW THINGS DOWN

"Strength and growth come only through continuous effort and struggle."
– Napoleon Hill

What do you think will help you learn a new language: a dictionary or an electronic translator? Many choose the electronic translator because of speed and convenience. Unfortunately, it slows down their progress and impedes their ability to memorize necessary words. Personally, I noticed I had to check a new word two to three times in a dictionary in order to remember it. The electronic translator did the thinking for me so I had to translate the same word many times and even after translating it eight or ten times it still wouldn't stick in my memory. Today, we can use GPS, Google, smart phones, etc., and they're truly great tools. However, they don't train us. By using them our skills aren't getting stronger, they're getting weaker. It's like going to the gym and asking someone to lift the weights for you in the hope that you will develop muscles.

In business, to become an expert, you must start by becoming an apprentice. There's no shortcut. Although, if you just read the headlines on social media, I'm sure you'll find countless examples of people promising you how to become rich instantly by following some simple, secret formula. The truth is, success requires hard work. You must also determine what kind of work is worth your effort. Far too many people fall into the trap of thinking that hard work will bring them success. All you have to do is go to a third world country and watch people working on farms to know this isn't true. They aren't rich but they work very hard.

In business, you will find story after story of people trying to scam others by overcharging and not delivering the value they promised. I have never met a person who successfully scammed others long-term. It's all about producing value in other people's lives. It's about delivering more than what people expect. It's about making someone's life better by creating value for those who need it. There's no shortcut. That's why so many businesses go bankrupt in a very short time. They don't want to take the time to build a brand with a solid foundation that represents value. When the storm hits, they get wiped out.

The struggle is real and in order to succeed you have to invest in yourself. It's by far the most important investment you will ever make. Create a map of what it takes to be successful. Go to school, take courses, read books, go to seminars, take on an apprenticeship, and acquire certifications. I don't know what it will take for you to become successful, but whatever it is you must make a point of identifying where you are, where you want to be, and the best path to get there. You don't have to learn everything, but you do need to know the things you can't outsource to others.

Creating a team is very important and hiring people will definitely be part of your success, but don't expect to just hire people to do things for you and hope they will create success for you. If you want success you have to become a leader, and leaders walk first.

There is one investment that will save you time, money, and lots of frustrations. It's the only "shortcut" that I know of that actually works. It's called modelling.

MODELLING SUCCESS IS THE NEW TIME MACHINE

"Remembering that I'll be dead soon is the most important tool I've ever encountered to help me make the big choices in life. Because almost everything—all external expectations, all pride, all fear of embarrassment or failure—these things just fall away in the face of death, leaving only what is truly important."
– Steve Jobs

Wisdom comes from experience. Experience comes from making mistakes and learning from them. The more mistakes you make, the wiser you will become. But, it's always better to learn from other people's mistakes. Coaching or mentoring can save you decades of mistakes. If you don't have money or connections to successful people, then books and biographies of those who inspire you is a great place to start.

There's access to almost anything we want at our fingertips and we can use NET (No Extra Time) to acquire this knowledge. Listen to audio books in the car, for example. Just add to your existing routine. Don't waste time by learning through trial and error, that's how our parents learned. We simply don't have that much time to waste. Time is our greatest commodity and it should never be wasted. You think you have time but the greatest lesson from death is that you don't. There's no reset button. There's no way of going back and there's no reason to waste your life on unnecessary activities. How much is your time worth? If you're wasting lots of time on a job you hate and at home you only watch TV to escape reality, then you are committing a slow suicide. That's right, your time is limited.

IF YOU KILL YOUR TIME, YOU'RE KILLING YOUR LIFE!

Don't try to be smarter than experts. Follow everything they do until you become an expert yourself, then you can start breaking some rules. Imagine, someone spent 20 years writing a book by gathering the best possible information from their life experience and then you read it in just a few days or sometimes hours. You can compress decades into days by learning from the masters. Can you imagine someone learning computer programming without any guidance? By the time they master the program, their skills will no longer be useful because a new program will take its place. We live in times when we no longer have the luxury of learning slowly. Businesses go bankrupt and get downsized and outsourced every day. Mostly, it's because they failed to innovate and hire consultants that could get them to the new goal faster. Someone else did and beat them to it. Today, making the best use of your time is what makes the difference between winning or losing, between succeeding and failing, between thriving and getting by.

The point of all this talk about time is simple: If you cherish your life and want to be successful, you must have a mentor or a coach. A mentor will give you a totally new perspective on things and could save you years of your life and lots of money in the process. No matter how smart you think you are, you're limited by your opinion and your own perspective. If you watch professional athletes, they all, without exception, have coaches. All famous actors, musicians, politicians, business owners, etc. have coaches and mentors. Many of them have multiple coaches at the same time simply because they know the value of it. Why reinvent the wheel if you can learn from someone who already made all the mistakes and walked the path you want to walk?

If you're serious about success, then you must immigrate to it. If you value your life, get a mentor.

Should you wish to learn more, contact Jacek Siwek at **immigratetosuccess@gmail.com** or visit his website at **www.immigratetosuccess.com**

Five Key Elements for Success

Shift to the Next Level

ALANA LEONE

There are moments in our lives when we have an opportunity to change our path, to explore in a new direction, and to step out into the unknown. Too often, doubts and fears can take hold in our lives, limiting the risks we take and the amount of success we can claim.

I want you to change all that. I don't offer this lightly. With the power of opening your mind to peak performance thinking, you are putting yourself on the path to generate the success you want in your life.

Now, to be clear, all of us have different definitions of success. You are already successful now in some areas of your life. Now let's take that to the next level.

It involves laser focusing on what you want instead of being stuck with what you don't want. By creating a drive to pursue your desires and ditching your limiting decisions and beliefs, your life will take on a whole new meaning. You leave the plateau and reach new heights. You feel energized! It takes stepping outside of your comfort zone and overcoming challenges instead of creating obstacles. It takes climbing one step at a time to the next peak.

As part of my work, I assist people to make the transition away from their fixed thinking and their inability to take advantage of the possibilities around them. Instead, I invite them to open their minds and explore what success they can claim through a shift to next level thinking. I give them the strategies, tools, and behaviors to be able to do it themselves.

Part of a mindset shift involves removing the sting of failure. I often tell my grandson, "What a lie of the mind it is to think you are going to start something brand new and you are not going to fail."

It is what you do with the failure that gets you to the next peak or leaves you stuck on the plateau. Take what you learn, implement it, and then do it again. When you take failure as feedback, it becomes less personal. If it is something you have decided you want, you will do it. Look at when you first learned to drive. Did you fail? If you are like me, then you likely did fail every day until the day you didn't. I didn't quit. You likely didn't either. I took what I learned and got back behind the wheel. This process is a strategy for success. It's a tool you already used in other areas of your life — only, you forgot.

Your mind likes to put you down and keep you safe. Mine too! Now I say thank you to my mind and make a shift to the next level. I have control over my mind, not the other way around. Too often, we attach negative emotions to failure. Instead, recognize it as a positive learning experience, one that is meant to assist your growth. There is potential in all of us to change, to alter ourselves and our circumstances. Too often, we allow our circumstances to turn into a much bigger obstacle, one that quickly becomes a blockade in achieving our goals and desires.

How can you push through the blockade? First, determine whether you are thinking with a fixed mindset or an open, curious one. As you explore your thinking patterns, you will be able to blast through the obstacles and blockades your mind has created.

As part of this journey, I am going to share with you the importance of five key elements for success. You can achieve success with these elements just by taking one step, then another — to shift to the next level.

PUSH THROUGH TO SUCCESS

When you operate with a fixed mindset, there are a few elements that come into play. One of the first is how you talk to yourself. In a fixed mindset, your self-talk tends to have a negative aspect to it. Time and again, you tell yourself that was a stupid decision. , You ask yourself "Why did you think you could do that?" or "Don't take the risk!" There is a lot of "No, no" and "Wait, wait" throughout that list.

Plus, when your self-talk is full of negativity, and on a constant repeat, then you quickly begin to believe what you are telling yourself. A vicious cycle starts, one that cannot stop unless you make a conscious effort to do so.

That self-talk also impacts your reality. After all, if you think you are not capable, then your subconscious mind is going to seek out the evidence of that from your surroundings. It reinforces that negativity.

Your subconscious mind is listening to the words you say. It believes that these words are what you want. That is why I cannot say it enough: Think and say what you want, not what you don't want. I catch myself doing this all the time. I frequently ask myself, "Is that what I want? If not, then change it right now!" Once you spend time focused on the positive or what you want, then you will see it leak out of your mind through your mouth. Then it moves from your mouth to your actions. It is a beautiful sight and sound. Once you experience it over and over, you feel amazing.

When you push through a negative mindset, you make the conscious choice to focus your thoughts around a positive viewpoint. There are many tools for your toolbox in the world today, and you have to be willing to use them. You gain the discipline to keep on top of it. Look at football or any sport you love. The coach is there every game and every practice to push through negative mindsets and motivate the team. The coach doesn't come at the first part of the year to give the team a pep talk and then nothing the rest of the year! He constantly pushes and reminds the team, "You got this!"

How can you make these new decisions? The first part of any new strategy is recognizing what decisions to eliminate. Recognize that eliminating one negative decision or belief means another positive decision of belief must replace it. Otherwise, within the vacuum, your old ways are likely to return.

Next level thinking is about pushing yourself to identify those unproductive patterns within your subconscious way of thinking and shifting them into what you desire. Often the best way to address limiting decisions and beliefs is through a conscious dig into your past.

Past experiences and decisions create limiting decisions and beliefs. In turn, that past creates a root cause, likely within the years of your life up to age seven. In fact, without learning from the past issues, you are susceptible to another limiting decision or belief based on the same root cause. Think of a tree with lots of fruit on it. You automatically assume that the roots of the tree are flourishing. However, there may be rot that is not visible to the naked eye. The same is true of your life. There may be root causes that keep you from flourishing but are not easily spotted.

Let's start with examining what root causes are and how to tear out those rotting roots and replace them with nourished, healthy roots for your life and your business.

ELEMENT #1 - ROOT CAUSES

First, let's start with how you are thinking now and the impact it has on your life.

We all have a story that starts with detailed events and ends pointing the finger at someone else, declaring them guilty of some misdeed. In many ways, this is the story of self. What you believe about yourself and others in your story gets ingrained further through a spiral of negative thoughts and actions.

The more we talk about this, the deeper it gets driven. At some point, the body starts to feel the emotions in other ways, such as sickness, depression, rage, and anxiety. A trip to the doctor for a pharmaceutical cure focuses on the ailing body, but not the root cause in the spirit.

As you think back to the main events of your story, I would like you to come up with an age when an event occurred. Are you two, four, six, ten or twelve? Now I would like you to think about how long you have been preparing and restructuring this story of the past into your conceptualized self. This part creates an identity. There is usually a lot of emotional baggage, often sadness, anger, fear, hurt, and guilt. You end up feeling trapped and making decisions based on those emotions. Thus, you create a pattern of self-sabotage or procrastination. You want the procrastination to go away, but it goes much deeper than just procrastination. The cause is deep in the soil and the roots, corroding and rotting them further.

It becomes a deadweight in your life, one that keeps you from pushing forward. How long do you want to be trapped by those emotions, the hurts, and the negative energy that comes from these stories in your life? How long is enough for you to hurt before you are done with it? When do you decide that it is time for you to have the freedom to push forward?

Our childhoods are not dictated by us, but by the people who surround us. Parents, extended family, and others impact who we are and the experiences that we have. Those experiences shape our beliefs about ourselves and who we are in the world. However, there are also those of us who grow up in situations based on past hurts. Those older adults do not know how to address their past hurts, so they pass those hurts onto their children. It becomes a generational hurt, one that has roots so deep it can be hard even to address them.

They have all done the best they can with their experiences. This reality may be hard to hear, and it doesn't give people a pass for being this way. However, they were that way, and now it is up to you to push forward and make different choices because you can see a different path. The best thing you could do to get back at them is to have massive success and joy.

Let the events in your past propel you to impact your present and future for good. You might want to break that cycle of negativity and rot. However, that can be difficult because you don't know any other way to think, feel, or behave. What do you do?

Our society is changing, and the next generations are determined not to carry that heavy emotional and mental baggage into the future. Their choice to address these issues or root causes means developing new tools. My passion is to share these tools with others for the next generations and our nations, thus transforming our world with information and education.

One aspect of shifting our thinking is in recognizing new teachings about how to harness the power of your mind. Some people were taught about the mind, how powerful it is, and how it helps to keep us safe. Some people were taught that we have control over the actions of our mind. We are not powerless over our thoughts. You are programmed with certain beliefs and values. The good news is, if you want to change the old programming, then you can.

Shifting your negative beliefs and useless values can take courage. In the end, however, it is a very cleansing experience. By that I mean, when you settle past hurts, you can address your emotional baggage and set it down for good. How can you set that past baggage down?

Part of that is based around the principle of forgiveness. When you forgive someone, you free yourself from any power they might have over you, mentally and emotionally. Forgiveness involves letting go of any resentment and refusing to allow them to hold you emotionally hostage. Often, while you might be hurting, they might not even still be thinking of you or even remember the hurt that they caused. That person might even justify it in their minds, believing that it was for your good.

In the end, you have the power to decide how long you are willing to let the actions of others impact you. It is up to you now to take responsibility in your choice to stay stuck or push forward. It is not always easy to make that decision and stick with it. Emotions can come into play, essentially sabotaging your efforts. When you choose a path and stick with it, then you find that shift in your thinking. The most effective way is to remove the emotion around the event and come up with some learnings. This process is what I have mastered. Do not let your mind come up with excuses. Rid yourself of the past burdens and fly free.

My passion is to give people tools to clear those emotions. It is important to remove the toxic negative emotion — the root cause — by filling your roots with a powerful positive emotion. You need to give yourself the tools to drain the emotion of a memory. Doing so will allow you to be at peace with those events and then push forward with your life.

Another important point is that you can have positive root causes as well. Those are the memories and emotional ties that helped you understand your purpose or gave you a belief system that continues to support you.

Positive roots can also be a way to connect with others. When you have a positive experience, it tends to color your day and make you more inclined to try and do the same for others. Shifting your thinking involves taking those positive root experiences and allowing them to help you gain a deeper understanding of yourself and to deal with others in a kind, generous, and loving way.

I love the metaphor of the tree. Roots are so critical to the life of the tree. Without proper care, then the tree will eventually die from a lack of food, water, and stability. Think of all the ways that your roots provide stability in your life. They ground you, give you a sense of the world you live in, and social rules that help you to operate in that world. Negative root causes can be damaging to your internal root system, thus threatening your stability and the means by which you can continue to grow and flourish in your life. Granted, it is possible to save the tree, but that means you need to do the hard work to address the rot. Addressing rot involves self-care and hard work, as well as creating new patterns that will nourish healthy roots.

Essentially, addressing rot can save the tree. Plus, when you take the time to care for your roots, both positive and negative, then you will find that your tree is healthier and more stable.

When you see a tree with toxic roots — the leaves are brown and sparse — there is evidence of compromised stability. It is dying a slow painful death. After some time, the tree will fall over in a windstorm. Move to a picture of a tall, healthy tree with strong roots. This tree will have a lot of leaves and be strong and confident in its stature. It will also have big, juicy, and excellent tasting fruit, and live a long, healthy life.

The healthier the roots, the more productive the tree and the more excellent the fruit. Your life can be the one you have always imagined, but only if you are willing to change how you interact with the world by addressing the various root causes within your background. I want you to be a healthy tree, not one with sparse and brown leaves, struggling to survive the windstorms of life.

Now you need to look at your roots. Are they healthy or can you detect some signs of rot? When you detect that rot, it is important to address it right away. Next level thinking means not allowing thoughts, emotions, and events to fester and cause further damage. At the same time, when you address those root causes, then you are dealing with the damage already done.

I want you to understand that it is possible to get your roots healthy and keep you growing and thriving. Next level thinking focuses on helping you understand yourself better, including why you react a certain way, and why certain situations trigger specific emotions. There are always root causes.

Addressing them will help clear the way to change how you react not only in these situations but in other stressful circumstances and wind storms.

I am passionate about helping individuals detect the rot in their roots and then ferret it out. Once you clear the damaged roots, the tree (you) can flourish and grow toward your goals and dreams without that dead weight. Part of that process is not only clearing the negative, but also helping new roots grow in place of those old roots.

Too often, people focus on those old root causes and make them the obstacle that keeps them from pushing forward and embracing new ways of thinking. However, when you decide that you will address those root causes and that they will no longer be obstacles, then you can begin to see the new possibilities that await you! You begin to look for new roots.

Recap:
- Root causes impact our beliefs and values, how we think, and our self-talk.
- Addressing root causes can leave room for new growth.
- Work with me to clear out your rot and clear the obstacles in your path.

ELEMENT #2 - NEW ROOTS

To be even more successful, you need to recognize the responsibility you have in your life to choose change. You are in charge and have the power to shift your beliefs and values. Your experiences give you valuable learnings, so you can reach out to expand and flourish. Your mindset controls your behavior. When you take the knowledge and leave behind the emotional sabotage, you will train your brain to search and keep busy looking for positive information.

It is like a puppy that is full of energy. When you aren't giving the puppy something productive to do, then it will eat your shoes. Keep your mind busy with actionable thoughts and productivity, thus training it to work for you and find even more creative ways to keep busy. Your mind will spiral up and not down. Give your mind something powerful to focus on.

Shifting your thinking can help you transition into the type of thinking that will allow you to envision a new path for yourself and then work to achieve that change. To have more success in all areas of your life, you need to recognize that you and only you have the responsibility of choice — and to change your environment. You are the one that has to move your foot forward to take that step.

I can help you decide where you want to place your foot, but you need to be the one to take that step. As you create new roots for yourself, it will be easier to push forward. Recognize that you are teaching yourself a new skill, one that is going to require you to step outside of your comfort zone. Like any new skill, it might feel awkward at first, but over time that awkwardness will fade.

I want you to stop for a moment and think about the language you use when trying to do something new. There are phrases that you can use which will indicate how successful you can be. When you start with a negative mindset and speak negatively about what you are attempting, then you are likely to find yourself giving up if it is not successful on the first try.

Too often, people focus on what they are doing wrong or they ask "why questions." For example, "Why does this happen to me?" Notice when you shift your mindset and start to create new strategies and processes, you begin to look at what you are doing that is amazing. Then you might start asking yourself, "How do I focus on expanding that positive energy?" Positive thoughts and energy attract more positive thoughts and energy.

Now, shift that language to more positive language. Do you see the difference in how willing you are to keep going in the face of challenges? How you talk about something and what you focus on about that item or experience can help determine if you will be successful or not. When you say, "I can get into this," it is positive. When you say, "I won't be able to get this done," it is negative. Pay attention to what you say. It is very important. The point of new roots is that you are changing your focus and how you speak about the events in your life.

I want to push you to step outside of your comfort zone and think about how you talk to yourself and how you talk out loud to others. What are you truly ordering up on the menu of life? If you are not clear and using clear, positive language, you are probably going to continue to find your goals thwarted or the delivery being less than what you had hoped to achieve. You think you are ordering a 12-course meal, yet you get back liver stew.

After taking my four years of training, I realized that I now had a skill that would help me push forward in my life and to create an amazing future for myself. I know how to talk to my goal-getter, and the results have been incredible. I want you to have the same experience. By taking the time to look at your mental language, you can find the patterns or places where communication is breaking down and create new positive processes.

It is up to you to create new roots and allow yourself to be at peace with your past, just as it was up to me to do that for myself. Once you put all the pieces into place, then the possibilities are endless.

When you are defining your new roots, you need to have a laser focus on what you want. Distraction can keep you from achieving what you want. If you find that you are distracted, remember that you do not have to stay that way!

Part of my pushy training is about pushing you to move past those distractions and to regain your focus. You have control over your thoughts. Consider your thoughts as leaves on a running river. If you are standing on the bank of the river, then you will see those leaves floating passed you. Your thoughts are also moving at the speed of a river, so you need to decide which leaf to grab.

That is how you need to focus, simply by picking one positive thought or idea and then giving it your full attention. When you focus on a pattern of negative thoughts, then you are going to find that type of energy coming your way. However, when you immediately decide to focus on the positive, then you draw that positive energy towards yourself.

Here are just a few examples of the types of positive energy that you can create with your thoughts: love, understanding, and compassion. It is about flexibility to focus and also to dream and live in a creative space.

Now that you have an understanding of how you can control your thoughts, you can identify the patterns that could be obstacles in your life. The obstacles are a tapestry of limiting decisions, negative beliefs and values, to name a few. These drive you to take action or not. If your drive in the past has allowed you to coast, then we need to push the gas pedal. Change involves making the move to throw the bags out of the trunk, thus lightening your load. Then press the accelerator to the mat and take off!

Recap:

- Shift your thinking from the negative to the positive.
- Take control of your thoughts. You have the power!

- Create a laser focus on what you desire to achieve.

Now, I want to shift your focus to the last three elements I will be discussing in this chapter.

ELEMENT #3 - PURSUE YOUR DESIRES

Align your life and business to your desires. We have looked in detail at the root causes and received the learnings and released the negative emotions from the events. We have created new roots and realizations. You are thinking about things differently and in a new light. Now you may have determined what you want and may even have a vague idea of how you are going to get there.

You may find that, now, you are ready to focus on how you are going to achieve the life you desire or even to focus on the fact that such a life is possible. Remember, use direct and clear language with yourself and others that defines a specific path. If you don't do this you might not get what you expect, even though you followed the path. Your words and phrases need to be in alignment with the possibilities. The various parts of you need to be integrated, and then you need to decide on a clear path.

As you sharpen your definition of the life you desire, you give your mind something to work with. Start by asking great questions of yourself and others. Get curious about what you like and what you don't. When you work at home, which tasks tend to go quickly, and which ones tend to drag on and on?

Define your strengths and weaknesses. They can help you see what areas might be creating challenges in your life that you need to address. How can your strengths work more effectively for you? What might you need to go learn more about to turn your weaknesses into strengths?

One of the best ways to truly define the life that you desire is to visualize yourself in the life you want today as if you already have it. Write out in a journal that ideal and desired life. Give it as many details as possible. Include what it feels like, sounds like, smells like, and looks like. See yourself there and then describe that image. Act as if it is today you have what you want. I am sure that you might have done something similar in the past, but now that you have looked at root causes, it is time to do it again. What you focus on only gets bigger as you get accustomed to taking those massive actions! Focus on the desire.

One caution about focusing on your desire is to not stay in the future all the time. It is a beautiful dance to be able to be in the present most of the time and also focused on the future at times. It is about putting the desire in the future with you in the picture and then being in the present to complete the tasks.

It is also about fun. Being in the present is fun. I will straight out start belly laughing in the middle of something, and people say, "It is her laughing time." That laughing time is catchy though, and others soon start to laugh along. It is also my process for bringing me back into the present. I enjoy floating around in the future, sometimes too often. The action happens in the present.

You want to have everything you ever dreamed of in your life. You and I only get one chance at this life. What is holding you back? What are you going to do about it? Clearly, throughout our discussion, I have identified some root causes that you need to consider, as they could be blocks. However, I have also shared a few points to help you address them. Now I want to connect with you to help you to shift your thinking and keep going on the journey at my website, www.pushycoach.com.

Recap:
• Define your desires.

- Determine what is holding you back.
- Don't stay in the future, but keep a foot in the present.

ELEMENT #4 - ACTION

All that I have talked about throughout this chapter has led to this element, the one regarding action. Too many of us focus on the fear of a situation, and that keeps us from acting. However, when you focus on what you want — I mean laser focus — that fear will go away. You will move forward, despite the fear.

You must choose your mindset. Success is a decision. Not having success is a decision as well. A positive mindset takes work. It's like working a muscle. The more you go to the gym, the bigger the muscle. The more you focus on your positive mindset, the better the chance of getting that desire. You make the desire bigger and brighter, bigger and brighter.

When you learn the pattern of clear focus, then your vision gets bigger, clearer, and brighter. Focusing on the future and then acting on that vision means you are focusing on the future and not on the past. It is a sure sign that you are growing strong roots and are ready to move forward.

When you do make strides forward and an obstacle gets in your way, or you fail at something, it could be easy to decide to quit. A lot of people quit and tell themselves, "I guess it wasn't meant to be."

Keep your power and the ability that you have to be successful. If you are starting to do something that you have never done before, why would you expect not to have obstacles or that you might not have failures along the path to success? It is unrealistic to think that way.

Put positive processes in your mind every day. Give your mind exercise. Going back to the coach story, you recognize that coaches are consistently telling you new teachings and giving you more motivation — not once, consistently! Doing small things consistently is the key.

People get busy doing tasks that have nothing to do with their desire and then the day disappears — a week, a month, a year, ten years. Act now.

Additionally, it is critical to have a support team in place to help you as you transition to your shifted life. This is why I love setting up Mastermind groups. Masterminds are where like-minded people get together to work on a clear direction and get the wisdom and experience from the entire room, not just yours alone. Who is in your support team? Think about the people you rely on for advice, encouragement, and motivation. Are they providing that or are they bringing out the negative and showcasing a critical spirit?

Recognize that to build a positive support team, you need to be willing to be a positive support to others. That quality will draw people of like-mind to you. Do not be afraid to let go of the people that are limiting you, despite your efforts to be supportive of their dreams. Perhaps letting go of that relationship will make room for greater opportunities, including the chance to meet new people who can join your inner circle.

My point is that I know you are going to achieve great things. Do you know it? Once you do achieve them, it is important to celebrate and express gratitude to help keep those positive roots nourished.

Recap:
- Take the first step to create success.
- Build a support team.
- Be supportive of others, and it will return to you!

ELEMENT #5 - CELEBRATION AND GRATITUDE

Probably the best part of achieving anything in life is the satisfaction of knowing that you accomplished what you set out to create. That can be the push you need to start a new project or create a new chapter in another area of your life. I always believe in celebrating your successes, as it can be a true source of motivation and inspiration. However, celebrations do not have to be limited to times when you accomplish something or are successful in an effort. Find at least one thing to celebrate everyday!

When I do my talks, I ask the group if they have celebrated themselves that day? I always raise my hand. My hand is often the only hand raised.

Why is this the case? You are so good at being hard on yourself that you are not good at celebrating yourself and your accomplishments. Without your struggles and obstacles, then you would not be who you are. You are an amazing individual, especially because of your blemishes and scars. Your marks say who you are, and they make you the strong person you are. That is something to celebrate.

The point is that celebrating yourself is meant to push you forward to the next level and shift your thinking to bring you the life you desire. Part of that process involves being grateful for what you have achieved already. Gratitude is something that you can pass on to others, and it creates a positive energy that only grows.

Part of celebrating yourself involves exploring what you enjoy and trying new things. When you find fun things to do, then they keep you in a great state of mind. You have the choice to create your day your way, so why not start as soon as your eyes open! Starting this way could be the most comfortable and rewarding process of your day.

Recap:

- Celebrate what you have accomplished.
- Be grateful for your abilities.
- Explore new things and step outside of your comfort zone.

SHIFTING YOUR THOUGHTS STARTS NOW!

Here is a 10-minute process for you to begin shifting your thinking first thing in the morning. Do it consistently. Before even setting your feet on the ground.

This process is known as the "Push through to your purpose" process. It is given to you from the The Pushy Coach®. I created this so that people can shift their thinking even before they put their feet on the ground first thing in the morning. When does the mind start with its noise? Right — first thing! Beat your mind and put in the shift of positive energy before your feet hit the floor. You can do this process even before you are out of bed or while you are still stirring. I call this process the easiest process because you are still in bed. You can begin to build healthy roots for your amazing life from the comfort and warmth of your own bed.

1. Decide and choose this time to not only wake up physically and emotionally, choose to wake up consciously and to live on purpose.

2. Set an intention for your day. Intentions are critical for taking action. Some examples to get you started.

   a. I am open to new positive experiences today.

   b. I experience myself of service to others today.

   c. I am 100 percent present and aware with others today.

   d. I experience myself healthy, wealthy, and unconditionally happy today.

3. Say three to seven gratitude statements. What are you happy about? Some examples to get you started.

   a. I am grateful for the sun.

   b. I am grateful for my family and/or friends.

   c. I am grateful to have woken up this morning.

   d. I am grateful for the fresh air today.

4. Celebrate one success from the day before.

5. Say, "I like myself. This day is the best day ever!"

6. Visualize great things happening today. Get up you amazing person.

7. Repeat the process daily.

The secret is to focus on what you want. With these few new things to do, even before you get out of bed, you will be creating a great add-on to the success elements that you are already making a part of your life.

To do something different — to break through your comfort zone barrier — is part of living your desired life. When you get proactive to your outcomes and desires and less reactive to limiting decisions, beliefs, unaligned values, and more, then you can truly move your life onto the path that allows you to have an amazing life journey.

You can say you didn't know before, but now you do know. To live and to pursue your desired life is a choice you can make or not. Taking action is a responsibility. Consider yourself pushed. If you need a bigger push, then contact me at www.pushycoach.com or ask us about our 1-year "Shift to the Next Level" coaching package and also how to get the bonus 5-hour "Breakthrough Experience".

I believe in tearing out the old roots so much that I want to get you a fresh beginning by taking the "Breakthrough Experience" before starting your Next Level Coaching to get you to the next level in your life. In the Breakthrough Experience, you can learn to release root causes, and in the "Shift to the Next Level" coaching, you can lock in new roots to pursue your desired life with action. Take action and celebrate yourself and others with gratitude.

I appreciate you, and I thank you for taking the time to read through and learn about next level thinking. With you here, it also helps me move forward to a new way of thinking. When you think about it, there is always a next level, and we can do it together.

To learn more about Alana Leone,
please go to www.pushycoach.com

The Yellow Lights in Life Matter, Reset and Go

JIM HETHERINGTON

*"If we did all the things we are capable of,
we would literally astound ourselves."*

– Thomas Edison

I stood staring into the eyes of a 700-pound tiger, hoping I would survive the encounter.

In my early 20s I had the privilege of working for the African Lion Safari in Ontario, Canada for five years. It was a thrill for me. I loved the animals and being outside. I guess I was good at what I did because in my second summer season there the manager walked up to the supervisor and myself and said, "Steve you're out. Jim you're in."

In other words, Steve was demoted and I was promoted. The manager of the park didn't like the way the supervisor was running his section.

There was no training and I had no experience. All of a sudden, I was responsible for lions, tigers, cheetahs, and bears. Oh my.

The next summer, my boss came up to me and said, "On my days off I want you to take my responsibilities."

He did not like doing radio interviews, TV interviews, or getting animals ready to be transported to another zoo. So, along with the responsibility of supervising a dozen or more staff, and overseeing about 1,000 animals on 800 acres of park, I covered for him on his days off. And guess what things were scheduled when my boss took his days off? You guessed it, interviews and the occasional animal that needed to be transported.

That's where the tiger comes in. Remember, I did not receive any real training; I learned as I went.

"We don't have enough time to get anymore help, we have to get this animal shifted," I yelled to one of my co-workers as we looked at this 700-pound tiger. It was sedated, laying on the ground in front of us as we tried to lift it from the ground and slide it into a transport cage.

Half an hour earlier, the staff and I were standing in front of the tiger's cage evaluating the situation. We had a 700-pound Siberian male tiger that needed to be transported to another park. So, it was my responsibility to come up with a plan, figure out how I was going to transport it, sedate it, and execute the plan — without any troubles or casualties.

I made the plan, got my staff together, and prepared the transport cage, which was on a trailer and raised about 6 inches off the ground. We had to back it up as close as we could to the pen, dart the animal, and, with our hands and ropes, slide it into the cage so that we could transport it. Seemed like an easy task.

I headed up to the office and unlocked the locker with the sedation medication and the dart gun. After I figured how much the animal weighed, I proceeded to calculate how much sedative I needed. I made the dart, grabbed the gun, hopped in my truck, and went back out to the park.

We stood in front of the cage and I waited for the ideal shot. I got a clean shot right in the back leg and we just stood and waited for the animal to fall asleep.

After about ten minutes we noticed that the animal was just sitting there staring at us. He was dopey and kind of grumbling a little bit. He was wavering back and forth, but he wasn't sleeping. It was then that I recalculated the amount of medication I sedated him with and realized that I underestimated his weight by about 250 pounds.

I raced back up to the office, got more medication, made another dart, came out and stood in front of the pen. I made another shot to almost the exact same spot. Then, we waited.

Five minutes later, the animal was flat, completely asleep. So we opened up the door and began to execute our simple plan.

Sliding him across even ground wasn't so bad. It was that 6-inch hump up into the transport cage that was the problem. I held his head and neck to keep him safe and to guide his shoulders up. What a struggle.

We repositioned ourselves so many different times, but still we could barely budge him up there. His shoulders were on the top of the cage, but we still had the rest of the body to come up with him. We just could not move him. One of the staff suggested he goes and gets more people to help. This started a bit of a debate.

As we were discussing, all of a sudden my hands turned and the cat was now staring into my eyes! Two things I noticed here. One the eyes were dilated which could have been from the drugs. The second thing I noticed was the eyes were green and I knew that was reserved for when Tigers get frightened or angry. Either way, I wasn't comfortable looking into these eyes. His mouth opened and he began to grumble and growl. At this moment I wasn't any happier than he was about our position.

I looked at the men who were around and yelled, "We don't have time to get anymore help, we have to get this animal shifted."

Within two minutes, we had that animal up – adrenaline kicked in and we slid him into the cage. We had no sooner got his back legs in, his tail in and closed the door, that he was sitting up inside this cage looking at us.

It's amazing what you can do when a tiger is waking up and you have no more time left. All of a sudden, what was impossible before became possible.

YELLOW LIGHTS ARE IMPORTANT

Many times in life, we run into situations that we are not sure how to deal with. When this happens, we may formulate a plan as we go with the hopes that things will work out. It's like driving along when all the traffic lights are green and then coming up on one that turns yellow. Then we have a decision to make: are we going to speed up and try to race through it, lock on the brakes, or just casually slow down and come to a stop?

Often, it's the same in our personal lives, our work lives, and our spiritual lives. A lot of us have that same approach when we encounter an unexpected situation that we are not sure of. We treat it like that yellow light. We could rush through without thinking about the consequences, we could jam on the brakes and stop everything because we can't handle it, or we could slow down and take the time to assess the situation.

Yellow lights are important in our lives. If we are in a situation, let's say in a business meeting that didn't go that well, the yellow light is the areas where we could have changed or done better. We evaluate the delivery. We evaluate what we said. We rethink how we approached the meeting or situation.

The problem is, sometimes when we get into those situations, we try to push our way through, like speeding up to get through the yellow light before it changes. We don't want to stop, we don't want to take the time to evaluate what happened. Often, we don't realize that maybe we were wrong or that there were things we needed to change.

The yellow light is the time to slow down and think about that meeting, think about that proposal, think about that relationship and how we interacted with that person. Look for ways we can adjust our thinking or adjust how we could have done it better. We need to look at the whole thing and be honest with ourselves. The yellow stands for "yell out." We need to speak out the frustration or tension we feel, and be open to adjust our thinking and our mindset.

The red light stands for "redo." We need to redo our thinking. When we reset our mindset and re-shift ourselves, we can decide how we will approach the situation if it happens again.

Red lights are a great time to reposition our hearts and redirect our attitudes. Red lights aren't always an inconvenience. They can be good for us too. By taking the time to really look at our heart and attitude, we can then move forward in a more positive manner.

Most of us have been frustrated with something or someone in the past. Imagine a time you were so frustrated you felt like spitting, and steam was coming out of your nostrils. Rather than giving in, you persistently pressed on, trying to win the argument or get your point across. You kept at the task with all the determination in the world, trying to overcome the obstacle. Finally, after a trying time, imagine you stopped and took a break. You got some fresh air, took a little walk, counted to ten, and took deep breaths.

To your amazement, as you went back to the situation it's like a cloud has lifted. All of a sudden, you were communicating, and it was actually working. You tried the task again and all the parts fit and worked as planned.

Was it a miracle? No. That's the result of slowing down (yellow light) and then stopping (red light) and seeing things in a new light.

Which leads us to the next step.

The green light. The green light is when you get going and decide that you are going to use that new mindset. The green light is you moving forward and doing things differently. This is where you apply what you have learned during the yellow and red lights.

It's the same in the relationships in your life. You can ignore what is going on or you can reflect and allow the relationship to become stronger. Let me give you a practical example.

How many times have you gotten into this situation? It's 7 o'clock in the morning, you got up late, and you are rushing to get everybody ready to go off to school and work. There are tensions and frustrations. You are getting under each other's feet. You part ways and everyone, including you, is in a sour mood. By the time you get to work, you are disheartened and ready to throw in the towel; you'd rather go back home to bed. Then, you go through the day thinking about it. You go over in your mind what went wrong, how it went wrong, and the awful things that were said.

The yellow light could be where you say to yourself, "How can I take a different approach to the way I spoke to my spouse, my children, or my significant other? How can I realign myself and speak out in a different way?"

The red light is realizing that you can't control that other person. You can't always control your work scenario or your home scenario, but you can control yourself and the way that you react.

I can control the way I speak out. I control my attitude. I don't have to allow my children or spouse to change my attitude. I can take responsibility for that and keep myself in check. The green light is to go and work on implementing the ideas you came up with.

YOUR SPIRITUAL LIFE

Sometimes in our spiritual life we can get frustrated with the universe, the world, and God because we don't think they are delivering what we desire. We don't think we are getting what we want.

That yellow light is recognizing that something is not right inside you or around you. That may be why you feel like you're being ripped off or not getting the answers that you want. Many times, those emotions are deep down. Instead of seeing the emotions, you see their effects.

The red light is to sit and realign yourself with your core values, core beliefs, and to see that God and the universe can be trusted. Maybe it is your beliefs that need to be strengthened. Ask for guidance. It will come in time. This is where belief comes in. Put action to your mindset and see it become reality.

THE CONSEQUENCES OF CONSTANTLY RUNNING THROUGH THE YELLOW LIGHT

One of the dangers of racing through the yellow light and ignoring that warning is that by the time you get through the intersection that light could be red. Now you are not going through a caution warning, you are going through a red light and there could be consequences.

From the driving side of things, you know what that is. If there is a police officer nearby, they could be hot on your tail and pull you over to give you a traffic violation. That could mean points and it could be dollars. It could be a lot of things. If you require that license for business, for travelling, or for making your income, you can only lose so many points before you are going to start getting into trouble.

From the life side of things, you may be ignoring warning signs. If you ignore these caution signs and yellow lights you are going to have to face the consequences.

One consequence in your business life could be continuing to not make sales. If you are unwilling to adjust your attitude or approach, then the consequence might be that you never get customers.

In relationships, if you keep plowing through thinking that there is nothing wrong and that yellow light is for someone else, the consequence might be a very unhappy, unfulfilled relationship. The frustrating and confrontational situations may never go away or get resolved.

If you think that everybody else is the problem, then you are never going to grow, or have a healthy and happy relationship. We need to take time, slow down, then stop completely and re-evaluate our approach to relationships before proceeding with a new attitude.

One of the dangers in life is we stop reading. They say the average person reads maybe two books through the rest of their life after high school, college, or university.

You get into the habit of just doing your job or going through your routines. If you don't adjust, the danger is you become stunted and don't grow and mature as a person.

Psychology teaches that by the time we are 35 years old 90 percent of thinking is just habitual. So if we don't interrupt that by continuing to build new habits and re-evaluate old ones (this could be replacing or re-surrounding old habits with new habits) we are in danger of staying the same person all the way through into our later stages of life.

About ten years ago, I had to step back and evaluate my life. I was at a time where I was working far too hard through the day. I was doing projects in the evening and working steady for seven days a week. Eventually, it caught up to me. I became depressed and tired and burnt out. It took me a long time to get myself back up there.

That period of time allowed me to reflect on what I was doing, how I was doing it, and how it was working for me. Quite honestly, my lifestyle wasn't working for me very well. That's what caused the burn-out. I had to acknowledge that I was striving for success and not getting there. I burned myself out in the process.

During that time of burn-out I was physically, mentally, and emotionally drained. I couldn't function. I was self-employed at the time, and I had customers that I had to serve and take care of. But I found that I was only able to work one or two days a week.

It took me a long time to get back up and I sacrificed a lot of income through that time because I had to surrender the contracts I couldn't fulfill. For me, it was a huge consequence that, because I had burned out, I couldn't fulfill the jobs that I already had.

Relationally, it was also very challenging. I have a very forgiving and very gracious wife and she was very patient with me at the time. I went through a period of six months where I said minimal words because I just didn't have the mental capacity or strength to verbalize my thoughts and emotions. It was too draining even to try.

THE TIME IS NOW

You need to step back and evaluate your life, daily, weekly, monthly, and yearly. You can only grow when you see what you must change. It is not other people's responsibility to change to what you want. You need to become more. You need to evaluate you.

Those yellow lights are the perfect time to slow down, pause, prepare to stop at the red lights, and take a reality check. What areas of your life need adjustment? What areas can you improve in? Remember that what you do affects everyone else, so by changing yourself for the better, others see it and it encourages them to do the same.

Don't look at red lights as an inconvenience anymore. If you need to stop at one STOP! Take the time to be grateful. Take the time to think about things in your life that you could change. Think of past encounters or meetings and think on how you might handle them differently next time. Don't rush through. Stop and reflect.

My tiger story at the beginning of the chapter? It is there to show that nothing is impossible. You may feel overwhelmed right now or at the edge of burnout. When you hit those times of life, it feels like life is impossible and that nothing will ever change. That is the way I felt, but I made it through. When things are at their worst, heed the yellow light and slow down to evaluate. If you keep speeding through, you will be stopped, whether it is by a police officer or by the other car that is trying to get through that same yellow light.

So, make the choice to slow down and stop. Don't plow through life trying to avoid every red light. As the old expression goes, 'life is a journey, not a destination'. Pause, stop, and proceed only after you have reflected, re-adjusted, and re-aligned yourself.

Would you like more resources? These extra resources will help you realize the relationships you want and to find the balance necessary to succeed. Go to www.YourRelationshipRescueCoach.com to check out other resources and articles that are available for you. Also, be sure to go to www.IncreaseTheLove.com to find other books that are available for you.

I would love an opportunity to sit down with you and discuss your unique situation. So please reach out to me at jim@yourrelationshiprescuecoach.com and let's book a complimentary consultation. During our 30 minutes, either in person or on Zoom, you and I will discuss areas that may be sabotaging your relationships, together we will create a crystal-clear vision, discuss a plan moving forward and send you on your way refreshed and re-energized.

During our session we can discuss ways to create an environment that better suits your needs and talk about ways to keep the momentum going forward. You and I will discuss ways that you can avoid colliding at life's intersection and discover how to apply principles that will help you navigate a healthy and balanced course.

Remember, it's not about how quickly you can blast through your day or your meetings, but it's about the quality interactions that you have along the way. If you will take moments to pause and reflect you may just find the days, weeks, months and years go smoother and more enjoyable over time.

To a life of enjoying the red lights,
Jim Hetherington

Your Life Energy

AMAL INDI

I have 20 years of experience in the tech sector and corporate banking. In my previous life in the "Rat Race", I was waking up every day and going to a job that provided well for me. After some major changes in my life (including a divorce), I started recognizing that I wasn't intrinsically happy. I would be going about my day filled with negative thoughts and emotions. It felt as though they were taking over in a way, and I recognized how they were beginning to affect every moment of my day and every interaction with those around me. I refer to these as "Thought Bugs", which I will go on to explain later. These Thought Bugs were almost like a computer virus, affecting all the thoughts or, as one may say, programming in my mind. After recognizing these Bugs and studying them in myself for many years, I began to draw strong conclusions about how I could create positive change in my mind. This positive change in my thoughts would eventually lead to me leaving the "Rat Race" and starting on the mission of my life to share my new paradigm with those around me. I believe that we can change our minds and create a positive and uplifting life, not only for ourselves, but for those around us. I would love to share with you the basics of what I discovered, a new way of examining our thought patterns and how to drastically shift the energy around you (your Aura) so that you can lead a fantastic life!

GETTING STARTED ON YOUR OWN JOURNEY

When was the last time you really felt 100%? When I say 100%, I mean you wake up feeling a general positivity in your mood, you are looking forward to a new day, your interactions with people feel good, and you walk around feeling a general sense of purpose even with the simple tasks of getting groceries or whatever your work environment. You may think that you have no say in how you really feel. That deep down, you cannot control your thoughts and emotions. I know that this is not true. I developed a unique way of seeing our minds and how deeply they affect our energy. Have you heard of life energy, such as positive energy, negative energy, Aura energy, and universal energy? Read on!

WHAT MAKES US HUMAN?

Each one of us is a biological marvel of different cells, tissues, genes. These are the many working pieces that come together to create our human body. What really makes us human in a whole sense? We each possess an in-depth energetic landscape that we can't deny. This energetic pulse is used by scientists and technicians daily to perform tests and create pictures of our bodies and their functions. Think of the neuroscientists that connect our bodies to electrodes and measure our brain waves. That's part of it. We can't deny there is a part of us beyond just the tissues of our muscles and bones.

Did you know that surrounding you right now is an energy field that is all your own? This energetic field is referred to as your Aura. This Aura can be the beginning of a life that you love. Every human being has an energy field around them. We cannot see this field with the naked eye. However, we can see this field with an Aura machine. It's true! I personally have had mine captured and what was reflected back to me (in terms of energetic levels) was what I was truly feeling.

Your Aura and the energy you radiate is 100% in your control. Some days, you might feel positive and good, while other days, you may feel more negative and lower. These are your energy levels. They can vibrate high or low. It depends on you and your thoughts. Remember, with improvements to your mind and thoughts, your aura energy field will continuously change, thus altering the life you are leading.

YOUR AURA

Over the centuries of humans existing and contemplating our existence, many have acknowledged the fact that we have an energy that extends beyond our skin and flesh, which can actually interact with the world around us. This is referred to as your body's Aura. The Aura refers to the energy around your body that can be affected from the inside out or the outside in. When it is strong, the Aura around your body can extend quite a way beyond the barrier of your physical body (your skin). It can also manifest as different colours, depending on the emotional mood of the person. For example, when you are

163

in a state of calm, then you will exude a white Aura. When you are in a state of anger, then you will exude a red Aura. Sometimes Auras may also be a combination of different colours. There is technology now that can show the colour and strength of someone's Aura. I have had mine checked. One day, it was light in colour and extended far beyond my body. This didn't surprise me as I feel I live in a state of calm, clear energy and my inner emotional landscape is positive. If you were to have an opportunity to get yours checked today what do you think the results would be? Strong and white? Or weak and maybe red? Maybe you feel like it may not show up at all.

This is what I want to teach you. This is my mission right now: To help you understand that you can empower yourself and create a strong, positive Aura that will not only affect your overall sense of well-being. It will affect your relationships, your business, and your life as a whole.

YOUR HUMAN SYSTEM

Through my own exploration, I began seeing and noticing a pattern in how my Aura was being affected by different things in my life. As I continued to study this in myself, it became clear to me that that there were specific things in play, and it was all rooted in my mind. Having a strong background in technology, I began to clearly see how our own minds behave like supercomputers. (Stay with me here!) Just like a super computer, we have our own operating system and the ability to run many programs at once. We are constantly juggling responsibilities, taking in the world around us, assessing how we feel, and determining what we need. The list could go on and on! Just take a moment right now: close your eyes and connect to all the "programs" open in your mind that are constantly running. Relate that to being connected to your own unique operating system of your mind. Now imagine that a computer virus was implanted into one of your programs and began affecting your thoughts. Computer viruses are designed to spread to all parts of a computer with the goal of eventually changing the computer, more often than not, making it completely dysfunctional. This is what can happen in your mind. A negative thought may enter your mind about something specific. Maybe a co-worker engages you in conversation about a rumour that someone is up for raise (one that you applied for) or on your coffee break the barista makes a mistake on your order and you feel it ruins your morning. I call these viruses of our thoughts Human Errors. In its most basic form, Human Errors can be outlined as the following emotions, or what I like to call Thought Bugs:

- Anger
- Suspicion
- Craving
- Comparison
- Low self-esteem
- Procrastination
- Getting stuck in negative thoughts

What it can be boiled down to is that these negative thought bugs can enter into your mind, which in turn creates negative energy. This leads to stress and a weakening of your Aura.

I'm sure you can think of a definitive moment, probably even within the last day or the last week, where you can see how your own errors were affecting your core system and negatively impacting the energy around you.

Luckily, we have a set of more positive emotions and various ways of reacting that counter the negative ones. I have identified these and aptly named them our Human Features.

Primary Human features that combat the errors include:

- Love and kindness
- Acceptance
- Forgiveness
- Courageousness
- Patience
- Authenticity
- Gratefulness

One can think of these features as a built-in tool box to combat negativity. This is always at our disposal! I want to help you identify where these positive emotions are in you, so that you may have access them and strengthen the energy that you are putting out into the world and your Aura.

Look, I am not a psychologist. I am not a therapist. I am, however, a believer in how we show up to our work and interact with those around us will have a deep impact on the life we are creating for ourselves. I have firsthand experience. I have taken myself from a place of negativity and darkness to a place of possibility. I have watched my newfound passions and work flourish, along with my relationships, personal and otherwise.

This is a different way of looking at things. This just isn't your usual "Be positive" message. This is connecting into the fact that as humans, we have a distinct design in place to help us truly create a good life for ourselves. The foundation of this is to truly feel happy and positive from the inside out, so that what we engage with is affected by our positive energy. Think of the last time you had an encounter with someone who you felt emitted a positive or happy energy? How did it make you feel? How did you react? You truly have the power to combat these negative thought processes (bugs) already in you! Don't you want to be the one truly living in your potential and sharing your positivity with everyone and everything in your life?

THE "AWESOME LIFE" IS WAITING FOR YOU!

Let's get down to business. Thanks for sticking with me. If you have continued reading to this point, then I want to applaud you! It means that you are deeply interested in living your best life.

Side effects of a mind free from negative Thought Bugs may include:
- General feelings of happiness and relaxation
- Genuine connections when meeting people
- A mind free from clutter
- A deep appreciation for the world and people around you
- High levels of productivity
- Willingness to learn new skills
- Gaining more contacts and connections with ease
- Feeling an authentic excitement for projects and self-development
- Being ready to rock your life!

These are just a few of the feelings available to you if you commit to removing negative Thought Bugs from your life, thus strengthening your energy and Aura from the inside out. I wouldn't be here today if I didn't do the work and experience the benefits of being on the other side of the process.

BRING LIGHT TO YOU

My hope for you is to learn how to identify your negative Thought Bugs and stop their process of multiplication. For you to empower yourself with positivity and strengthen your aura. For you to leave feelings of depletion behind and bring your energy back to 100%. For you to share your positive energy with the world and make it a better place!

Never forget: An Awesome Life is within your reach at all times. I believe it. In fact, I will go so far as to say I know it is. I have taken my own life and made it awesome by taking all I have outlined in my work and applying it to myself. Now it is your turn to turn up the positivity in your life and let your Aura shine!

I encourage you to check out my website, www.happinessmountain.com, to receive a free guide on removing your negative energy. In this guide, you will also be given a sneak peek into the app I am developing. The Happiness Mountain™ app will quickly become your new best friend! I developed the Happiness Mountain™ app to be a way to actually track those negative Thought Bugs and coach you to clear your worries and boost your energy levels! By giving you this important tool at your fingertips, I know you will be able to strengthen your energy and basically start living a more happy life! If you haven't guessed already, I love technology and its possibilities for enhancing our lives. I can't wait for you to be one of the first people to try this app and reap its benefits right away at www.happinessmountain.com/app.

BRINGING LIGHT TO YOU SO THAT YOU MAY BRING LIGHT TO THE WORLD

Now that I have given you some insight on how you can truly change your life by changing your own energy, I want to share the ways that Happiness Mountain™ can help you begin to apply these concepts. The process of understanding, application, and execution is key when committing to changing the way your mind functions and, over time, changing your aura.

Now that you know you have the power to change your life via your thoughts, I wonder why you wouldn't want to act now to change your life. Your own personal idea of an awesome life is within reach! I left behind an old way of living and being in order to start on a new path. I am confident that you have the power to do that for yourself as well. We all just need a little help. To be honest, I wish I had connected with these deeper levels of understanding regarding my thoughts and how they affect my life earlier. However, as we all know, timing is everything, especially when it comes to your advancement on both a personal level and a business one. Take this as a sign that it may be time for you to dive into these deep changes. The techniques, once you really begin to understand them, are quite straightforward. I know that you live a busy life and are striving to do your best. However, it takes commitment to change. Why not start now?

Happiness Mountain™ can offer you many tools to get started and help you dive deeper. The first step is easy! I encourage you to head over to my website www.happinessmountain.com to sign up and stay connected to the developments in my work. You will automatically receive an easy to follow guide on how to remove your negative energy, which will be delivered right to your inbox! You will also be given an automatic sneak peek into my app.

THE HAPPINESS MOUNTAIN™ APP

I am constantly inspired by how we connect online through different platforms and technologies. I believe that this can be the start to a great change in how we grow and develop. I designed the app as a convenient way for you to connect to your energy boosting practices on the go. We all spend some time on our phones scrolling and engaging on different platforms. Why not invest that time mindfully instead of mindlessly? The Happiness Mountain™ app, www.happinessmountain.com/app, helps you do that by having the tools you can utilize to boost your own positive energy available at any time!

Features include the following:

- Troubleshooting what is worrying you and replacing that worry with positivity

- Ways to resolve disputes without creating negative energy and affecting your Aura

- Aura boosting activities you can do on daily basis, while tracking your progress with your own private point system

- An emergency toolkit for handling sudden negative situations

- An easy guide to all the Thought Bugs and how to handle them available at a touch of your screen, so that you may continue to learn how you can change your thoughts to more positive ones and keep your positive energy high!

HAPPINESS MOUNTAIN™ FOR KIDS

Calling all parents and anyone who takes care of children! This work isn't just applicable to more mature minds and bodies. It can start when we are young! I am in the process of finishing development on a series of books for children that will cover all the core concepts of my work and Happiness Mountain™, so that we may share these valuable tools and concepts even with the developing minds of the next generation. Of course, there will be interactive games for children as well, because as we all know that some of the best learning happens when we are having fun! This goes for adults too, don't you think? Stay in the loop by connecting with me at www.happinessmountain.com.

MY NEXT BOOK

I am ready to dive deeper and share with you even more in my new book, *Happiness Mountain™: Double Your Happiness, Awesomeness and Spirituality*. In the book we are going to explore deeper than ever before. *Happiness Mountain™* will go more in depth on how you can harness the three levels of energy (Positive/Negative, Aura and Universal) to change your perspective and unlock your perfect life. I want to share with you the techniques and deep processes that will affect all aspects of your life. Remember those 'Negative Thought Bugs' I was talking about earlier? In my new book I will teach you not only how to eliminate them, I want to teach you how to protect yourself from future encounters with 'Negative Thought Bugs' therefore truly creating change in your life for the better. You will also learn techniques on how to recharge your energy, boost your aura and use your new skills for resolving conflicts and affecting your business.

I want you to harness the power of your personal Positive & Aura energies, learn to dance with the Universal energy that is always at your disposable and be able to live at a level of existence that falls in line with your ideal, perfect life. Take a look at the *Happiness Mountain™* diagram on the next page. You can define your perfect life as living with a high level of inner peace, the level of inner happiness. Your Awesome Life and Spiritual Life revolves around being of service to others and helping others. You can live a combination of all levels of the *Happiness Mountain™*. Whatever you personally define as perfection is where you have the power.

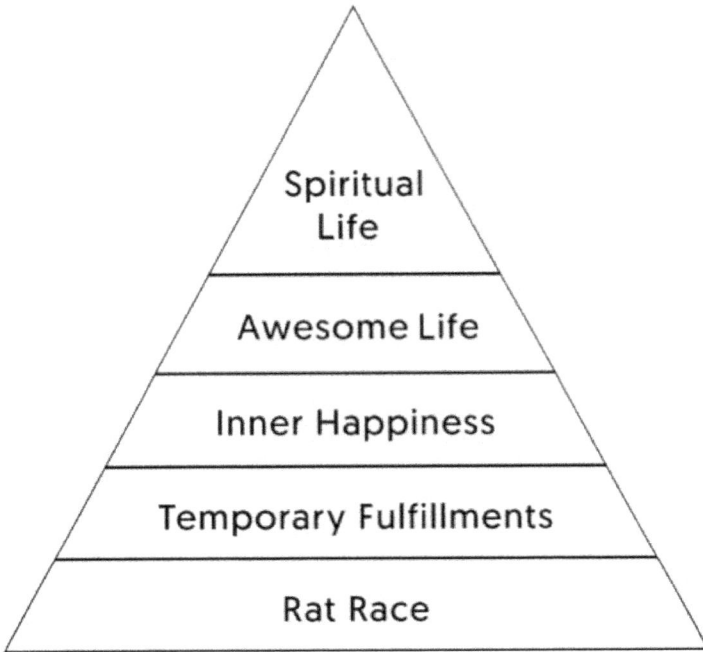

Happiness Mountain™ created by Amal Indi

Some might argue you cannot have a perfect life. I say you already have a perfect life and it is blocked by negative energy from coming into full fruition. This negative energy can be existing as a low self-esteem bug or a comparison bug. You may define perfect life as comparing to others. You may try to achieve things with craving energy. Please remember: You are already whole, complete and perfect. You cannot access your full power because of the negative energy being generated by your thoughts. When you learn to remove those negative thoughts as I teach you in *Happiness Mountain™*, you will realize how much power you have in life. This will be your turning point to harness the energy to power-up your personal, business and spiritual life! In the book I will give you all the tools and techniques to accomplish that. After reading my new book *Happiness Mountain™* you will be able to shift your life to a new paradigm that is not only accessible but exciting. How do you think it will feel to lead a perfect life? Can you think of even one thing that may change for the better if you decided to investigate how you could crush your negative energies, enhance your positive energies and essentially eliminate future worries from your life? ... Wow! I am excited for you just thinking about it myself! I know the profound changes it created for me in my life and I look forward to hearing how it affects yours.

YOU CAN LEAD AN AWESOME LIFE

My hope for you is to learn how to identify your negative Thought Bugs and stop their process of multiplication. For you to empower yourself with positivity and strengthen your aura. For you to leave feelings of depletion behind and bring your energy back to 100%. For you to share your positive energy with the world and make it a better place!

Never forget: The Awesome Life is within your reach at all times. I believe it. In fact, I will go as so far to say I know it is. I have taken my own life and made it perfect in my eyes by taking all I have outlined in my work and applying it to myself. Again, your negative thoughts may say your life is not perfect, which might include your low self-esteem, cravings, or comparison bugs blocking you. Don't let these bugs create negative energy. Instead, clear them and power-up the personal, business, or spiritual aspects of your life. Never forget you have the power over your own mind- NOT your negative Thought Bugs. Now it is time to power-up the positivity in your life and let your Aura shine!

I encourage you to check out my website, www.happinessmountain.com, for the opportunity to stay connected to the global community of people who have already begun to use this work to boost their positivity and create their

Awesome Life in their personal, business, and spiritual domains. I can't wait for you to begin using The Happiness Mountain™ App to start training your energy to stay positive and even get stronger. Of course, I encourage you to visit www.happinessmountain.com to stay connected and be in the know as to what is coming down the pipeline with this life changing work.

I have dedicated my life to bringing these concepts and work to you. I know you can change your energy and begin to not only affect your own life, but the entire world. I believe deeply that when as many people as possible align their energy to a higher, more positive state, then we can truly make a collective difference. Let's start today!

Amal Indi lives in Vancouver, Canada, and is the founder and CEO of Happiness Mountain™ Inc. After 20 years of working in technology and corporate banking, Amal is on a mission to give people the possibility to live with their full potential in their personal, business, and spiritual domains. He has found innovative techniques and tools to remove negative energy and power up your personal life, business life, and spiritual life. Ultimately, you can make the world a more awesome place for everyone. He believes that technology has the potential to transform the minds and energy of people and facilitate change. Amal wants to help people around the globe live a positive and enriching life through the energy-based tools and techniques of this innovative system he has developed to strengthen your energy and help you live a life full of happiness and potential. Find his story and work at www.happinessmountain.com.

Big Business Selling Strategies For Small Business Growth

GARY THOMPSON

T he vast majority of small business owners, whether they offer a service or make and sell a product, are good at what they do. But, being wonderful at something doesn't automatically translate into being wonderful at selling or marketing it. Most small business owners lack the skills they need to manage successfully and grow their businesses, which is probably why so many of them fail during their first few years.

There are two key issues that are problematic. The first is that today, many small business owners come out of corporate environments. After 15, 18, or 20 years, they decide it's time to quit the proverbial rat race and start doing something they actually like, hopefully, love to do. If you're one of them, you know that it's scary at first. It's hard to get a new business off the ground, especially if you are used to being part of a team. In a small business, you're largely on your own, with no accounting, marketing, or sales department for support. It's all up to you.

So, you start wearing about 12 different hats, doing all kinds of tasks on your own, from cleaning the floors in the morning to shutting everything up in the evening. Instead of spending your day doing the one thing you started a business to do, you move from chore to chore. Plus, when you are that busy doing, you never have the time to think about marketing and growing your business.

Often, the hardest task you take on is salesperson because, at some point in the conversation, you have to talk about money. It's not necessarily difficult to share your passion for the business or talk about the wonderful things that your product or service does for the customer, but closing the sale and discussing the price can be truly uncomfortable. Even someone who has been in sales at another company can still feel some level of guilt about asking for an order at the retail price when it's for themselves. And that's a huge impediment to being an independent business owner. It's crucial to learn how to sell your product or service for what it — and you — are worth.

It's not a matter of garnering selling expertise or knowing what you know. Unfortunately, knowing isn't enough. You must also believe it, and believe in yourself. You need to understand and respect your own worth, as well as the worth of your product or service. If you can learn to sell without feeling like you are begging for money, then you can grow your business as opposed to just running that business.

Of course, first, you have to get to the point when you are running your company, not just working in it. Once you start generating more income by closing the sale more often, you will have the funds to start hiring people to handle the tasks that are diverting you from being a real owner. It's not as easy as sounds because, once you eliminate the classic excuse for not delegating ("I'd love to hire somebody, but I can't afford to"), it is time to face the underlying reasons why letting go of the little things is so difficult.

In many ways, this is more a personal decision than a business one in that the business reason is obvious: your time is worth more than what you would have to pay others to do the bookkeeping and buy the stationery supplies. The hard part is making the psychological shift that will allow you to trust other people to do as good a job as you can. If you can get over that hump just once, it will become easier each time you do it.

Coaching both corporate and small business clients has helped me codify a process for overcoming these all too common personal issues that keep people from realizing their full business or career potential. It starts with developing, cultivating and maintaining your sense of business-related worth, and then delivering the story of that worth in a compelling and believable manner. This chapter provides an overview of the five key things on which you will need to focus.

FIVE POWERFUL ELEMENTS TO LONG TERM BUSINESS GROWTH

1. Craft Your Story

The most important thing you need is your story, which means understanding who you are, what you stand for, why you are doing what you are doing and with whom you are looking to work. The key is focusing on the why. You may already be familiar with the best example of building and maintaining a compelling story, but it bears repeating because the Apple case study is excellent at making the point.

The company has done an extraordinary job, and it isn't necessarily because their products are any better than anybody else's. The company has an ethos, an approach that involves going well beyond the status quo, especially as it relates to customer service. In developing its story, Apple has given itself a huge advantage over other corporate cultures, one that draws people to the company. That advantage is the why, as in better customer service is the reason why to buy an Apple instead of a computer from one of its competitors.

A lot of small business owners lose or forget their why when they get involved in the day-to-day running of their companies. They forget why they are doing it, whatever it is, because they spend all their time actually doing it.

2. Create an Experience

Remembering your why helps you understand, envision and create the experiences your clients are going to enjoy from their interaction with you. Your product may work better than others of its kind, your customer service may be superior, the sales experience easier and so on.

3. Build a Narrative

Your narrative is a personalized version of what marketing experts call a positioning statement. It tells much of your story in that it puts forth a picture of who you are and what you're doing, and summarizes the benefits of being one of your clients. Since you are the one who will be telling your narrative, you need to feel comfortable with the words and the thoughts behind those words. You need to know and feel that you are telling the truth. It's important that the narrative you put out makes sure you're seen as the person you want to be, and that your customers' actual experiences support your narrative.

4. Be Selective

Trying to appeal to any and everyone is a marketing strategy that may work for large corporations with products that actually appeal to everyone, but it is a tragic mistake for small business owners. Think of it in terms of someone going door-to-door, trying to sell magazine subscriptions. That's basically what you're doing when you sit at your desk with a phone in your hand, calling a list of cold prospects. The same is true when you take the networking route, drop leaflets or run blanket advertising. The process is archaic and makes for extremely hard, time-consuming work. Worse still, it is soul destroying.

There are better ways of finding clients and customers, but they only work when marketing and sales genuinely work together. The concept of true cooperation between the two may feel foreign if you come out of the corporate world, where marketing and sales are separate entities somewhat in competition with each other. In fact, and the way it should work, marketing generates leads, and the salespeople convert them.

Your marketing efforts are to there to help people raise their hands and say "Yes, I'd like to talk to you." When there has been prior interaction with a lead who has self-identified themselves as interested in your product, the conversation is totally different than it is during a cold call. There is much less pressure put on you to justify the cost of your product, and that lessens or removes the guilt about discussing money. Distancing yourself from lead generation is also essential to better managing your time and your efforts. The time to step into the process is when a viable lead has been identified and engaged.

5. Know Your Numbers

When marketing and selling are working in tandem, you can trace the conversion process and its associated costs, from reaching someone and getting them to self-identify through to the final sale and the amount of that sale. Tracking these figures along with the lifetime value of a customer will allow you to determine how much it costs to acquire a new client or customer, as well as the value of an average customer. This will allow you to confidently set your marketing budget for attracting new customers and long-term growth.

IT'S EASIER WITH HELP

As discussed earlier in this chapter, most small business owners already find themselves trying to do it all on their own. Delegating some or all of the everyday activities can be a huge help in freeing up your time to begin rethinking the marketing and selling plan for your own company.

However, if you are like most people, you will soon see that there is a big difference between knowing what to do, understanding what activities go into doing it, and actually doing it on a regular basis. Everything in life takes a bit of a learning curve and enough practice on a regular basis so that you feel comfortable doing things in a different way. The process is the same for any new beneficial habit; you need to keep feeding it and watering it, much in the way you would water and feed a sprout until it becomes a healthy, growing plant.

The good news is that you don't have to go through the process alone. A good advisor can guide you through the learning curve and help you manage the time commitment involved so that you don't end up putting too much pressure on yourself. An advisor can also help you hold yourself accountable in terms of getting things accomplished. That's something that just about everyone struggles with in most areas of life, but especially so in business — and even more so when you are running and trying to grow your own business. Perhaps most importantly, a good advisor knows how to help you work through any of the "I'm not good enough" feelings and insecurities that affect just about everyone at some time.

If you would like to learn more about what goes into taking these five steps at Gary Thompson's Workshops, please visit www.ThatTallGuy.com